The husband arrives home around 7 o'clock, exhausted from his day at the office. He has spent his day dealing with people and their problems and has had it up to the eyeballs. He wants to hide from everyone—including (especially?) his family.

Of course, the wife has also been up to her eyeballs in people and their problems all day, whether at a job outside or at home with the children. Although she has her own needs for privacy and quiet at night, most wives do want "something more" from their husbands in those hours when they come together.

He experiences her demands as more pressure. He retreats. She comes back at him with greater demands. He retreats further. She becomes hysterical, maybe abusive. He lapses into complete silence, total passivity. She goes wild. The battle escalates. This self-defeating pattern continues and gets worse. The pattern can last years. Lifetimes.

BUT THERE ARE SOLUTIONS...

# Passive Men, *Wild Women*

Pierre Mornell, M.D.

BALLANTINE BOOKS • NEW YORK

*To the memory of my father*

# Acknowledgments

Few ideas are translated into print without some rather crucial assistance.

Therefore, I would like to thank Joni Evans and Peter Schwed at Simon and Schuster. From the beginning they offered ongoing encouragement and editorial direction. Indeed, their ideas and enthusiasm made not only for an enjoyable collaboration among author, editor and publisher—but also their input made for a better book.

In addition I am grateful to Don Congdon, an extremely busy literary agent, who was never too busy to return a phone call or offer advice. He always did so with that rare combination of promptness, courtesy and common sense.

I am also indebted to those good friends and colleagues who read an earlier version of the manuscript and offered numerous helpful suggestions: Alexandra Botwin, Ph.D., Wolfgang Lederer, M.D., Jane Wheelright and Joseph Wheelright, M.D.

There's one final note of thanks. Over the past few years the men and women I've seen in my office have made an indispensable contribution to what follows. Although they must remain anonymous, these individuals have helped me not only to define problems, but to discover solutions. More importantly, they have also demonstrated a remarkable degree of courage under stress. At especially difficult periods in their lives, they've struggled against great adversity. By personal example they've repeatedly proved that problems can be overcome and change is possible.

No words of acknowledgment could adequately express my admiration for these men and women. To each of them I am not only admiring, but profoundly grateful.

*Pierre Mornell*
Mill Valley, California
Fall 1978

# Contents

# Introduction

In January of 1977 I gave a lecture entitled "Passive Men and Wild, Wild Women" at a local college. I spoke the same week that *Roots* was being shown on television. Consequently, I briefly wondered if I'd be speaking to a handful of people in an empty auditorium. I shouldn't have worried. The college was in Marin County, California, where there is one divorce recorded for every marriage. Four hundred people were awaiting my talk.

I spoke for about forty-five minutes and answered questions for another hour. By 10 o'clock it seemed clear that I'd struck a responsive chord with the audience. It was as if I'd hit a raw nerve. Or so I thought that night.

Aside from the audience's questions, however, there was no further reaction to my remarks. A month later I did receive one response from the San Francisco correspondent for the *Manchester Guardian*. He'd heard about my lecture and asked to interview me. He then wrote a lengthy article from an Englishman's point of view on what he called "The Latest Discovery of American Psychiatry—Passive Man!"

His article appeared in London on April 28, 1977. Accurately subtitled "Weak, Silent Types," the story was immediately picked up by the wire services. In America it hit the front pages of newspapers in Denver, Chicago, New Orleans, Atlanta, New York, Rochester and Iowa City. It even made news in San Francisco, which is ten miles from where I'd given my original lecture. Of course, the title had again been changed. It was now called "Why So Many Marriages Are Foundering."

Subsequently, I was deluged with phone calls and letters. A British psychiatrist wrote that he'd found the same syndrome in England. A man in southern Australia wrote that he fit my description perfectly, but what could be done? Two publishers inquired about translation rights in German and Spanish. In October I was invited to present my ideas as the keynote speech before the American Association of Marriage and Family Counselors. Suddenly, "Passive Men and Wild, Wild Women" had become a hot subject.

Why?

My hunch is that I *had* hit a raw nerve. By chance I'd stumbled onto a phenomenon that was at once universal and troublesome and obvious.

I say "universal" because of the international response to that London article. "Troublesome," because my ideas went against all the current clichés and popular jargon about male and female roles. (Maybe that's why newspaper editors kept changing my title. Calling women "wild" these days was definitely troublesome.) And "obvious," because I'd finally said aloud what everyone had known secretly for years.

Parts I to IV of this book are an expanded version of my original lecture. Part VI includes a review and my conclusions. Part V is a series of questions which have been asked by audiences as I've spoken around the country. Clearly, these audiences have shared what all of us have known in secret for years.

What was the secret?

In our own homes, most of us "men"—we would-be emperors—have no clothes. We are passive and that drives our women crazy.

# PART I

---

# The Problem

•

*We have met the enemy and he is us.*

Pogo

Over the last few years I have seen in my office an increasing number of couples who share a common denominator. The man is active, articulate, energetic and usually successful in his work. But he is inactive, inarticulate, lethargic and withdrawn at home. In his relationship to his wife he is passive. And his passivity drives her crazy. In the face of his retreat, she goes wild.

Webster's defines these two terms as follows:

*Passive:* Inactive, yielding, taking no part, submissive, acted upon without acting in return.

*Wild:* Not easily restrained, angry, vexed, crazed, in a state of disorder, disarrangement, confusion.

Of the wives I've seen in therapy none are actually crazed or disarranged, but a great many are certainly angry, vexed, and confused. They're also highly intelligent, talented women of all ages who have become super unhappy in their marriages. No doubt that's why I see them in my office.

The husbands are also highly intelligent, extremely likable, and, at least on an economic level, making it. They work hard in their business and professional lives. They're excellent providers. (They almost have to be good providers to maintain our astronomical standard of living.) But, as I said, active as they may be at work—they seem incredibly passive at home. They are increasingly impotent, literally and figuratively, with their wives. And they silently retreat behind newspapers, magazines, television, and highballs in the home. Or they perhaps not-so-silently retreat into affairs, weeknight appointments, and weekend arrangements outside the house.

Let me briefly describe a typical evening at home for such a couple:

The husband arrives around 7 o'clock exhausted from his day at the office. He has spent his day dealing with people and their problems. He has had it up to the eyeballs. Maybe even to his hair roots. He wants to hide from everyone—including (especially?) his family. He has a nonconversational drink or two, silently reads the paper and wolfs his dinner down. He pays only token attention to his wife, maybe a little more (or less) to the kids, and then withdraws behind TV's Monday night football or Tuesday night's movie. Remaining semiglued to the television set through the 11 o'clock news, he comes to bed eventually with his wife usually already asleep.

Variations on this theme of a man's need to hide include: His not coming home *until* the 11 o'clock news (with all of its obvious implications); or his having three drinks before dinner and a bottle of wine with it, so that he falls asleep at 9 o'clock while his wife stays up for the late show.

Of course, the wife has also been up to her eyeballs in people and their problems all day. Big people if she has spent a number of hours at a job outside the house. Little people if she has been home all day with children.

Although she has her own needs for privacy and quiet at night, I've found most wives—at least a majority of those who seek my help for their troubled marriages—do want "something more" from their husbands in those hours when they come together.

This need for *something* more is directly or indirectly conveyed to the man. Basically she is saying, overtly and covertly, "Give me something I'm not getting."

He, in turn, experiences her demands (for longer talks, or an honest expression of feelings, or spending more time with the kids or her, or his being more active in sharing the domestic load, or her desire for better sex) as MORE PRESSURE. (Pressure he needs like a hole in the head.) And in the face of that pressure, direct or indirect on his wife's part, he withdraws. He retreats. He lapses into sullen silence.

What is her reaction?

As I said, it was her husband's withdrawal that made her furious in the first place. So, more agitated, she comes back at him with greater demands for "something he's not giving her." This causes him to retreat further. She becomes more pressured, even abusive. He retreats further. She becomes hysterical, bitchy. He lapses into complete silence, total passivity. She goes wild. The battle escalates. The self-defeating pattern continues and gets worse, if that's possible. And it is possible. The pattern can last years. Lifetimes!

Variations on the theme of a wife going crazy include: Her drinking too much, eating too much, getting depressed, having an affair or simply withdrawing herself by either shutting up or getting out. For example, she starts going to three night meetings or two evening classes a week. She can also take out her frustrations on the children or the dog. And not infrequently, she does.

What's going on here?

·

| Higgins: | Why can't a woman take after a man? |
| | Men are so pleasant, |
| |    so easy to please; |
| | Whenever you're with them, |
| |    you're always at ease. |
| | Would you be slighted if I |
| |    didn't speak for hours? |
| Pickering: | Of course not. |
| Higgins: | Would you be livid if I |
| |    had a drink or two? |
| Pickering: | Nonsense. |
| Higgins: | Would you be wounded if I |
| |    never sent you flowers? |
| Pickering: | Never! |
| Higgins: | Why can't a woman— |
| |    be like you? |

*"A Hymn to Him"*
*My Fair Lady*

Why can't a woman be just like a man? And conversely, why can't a husband better understand his wife's needs at night?

One of the reasons relates to a conflict that I also hear from the majority of couples who fit this description of a withdrawn husband married to an unhappy wife. That conflict involves the fact that there is a basic difference between the man's needs and the woman's needs at night. Frankly, I think this difference is the *key* to why men are so passive and women wild in this kind of relationship. It is the crux of the self-destructive nature of such a marriage. It is also one of the most basic and least understood reasons, I believe, for

4

our well-publicized and recently popularized divorce rate.

What is that difference?

It is simple. The most important part of the man's day—earning a living—is over when he hits the front door at night. However, a crucial part of the woman's day—making a connection in the relationship—is still to come.

Whereas a man may get his sense of worth from work, his wife needs a sense of her worth not only from her work, but also from her relationships. At home the husband needs to tune out. His wife needs to tune in. Beyond her own needs for privacy, the woman needs emotional contact with her man.

Personally and professionally, 95 percent of the couples I know describe this difference in their marriage. It is a profound difference, and I believe it is one of the most overlooked realities of married life.

I hear this male-female difference from the wife, whether she works outside the home or in it. I hear about the difference from the husband. I hear it in individual hours and conjoint sessions.

One of my steps in therapy is to explain that differences between men and women, if unrecognized, can lead to trouble. And I often start with a basic difference between people, men and women alike, that we can all understand.

Take the difference between "night people" and "morning people." More specifically, I know a working wife who starts her day at sunrise, and yet her musician husband doesn't begin his day until after sunset. Such a couple with different time clocks know the problem of denying their differences. If differences are ignored, the couple are on a collision course day in and day out.

Another example is a stockbroker husband who invariably wants to make love at 6 in the morning to his wife, who usually sleeps like a log until 8 or 9 A.M.

They're like trains passing in the night, always two or three hours off schedule.

I know an early-rising wife who describes her husband as a pathological night person in his sleeping pattern. His disease is so severe, in fact, his wife says that if a burglar were robbing the house at 5 A.M., it would be impossible to wake her "protector." By the time her husband got out of bed, put on his glasses, found a flashlight, and placed his feet firmly on the ground, the robber would have been long gone.

Even when recognized, this problem of different biological time clocks is an extremely difficult dilemma for most couples to solve. But unrecognized, it creates an absolutely impossible situation.

If we ignore differences, each person takes the other's inner sense of time personally. Falling asleep (or not waking up) is seen as a personal rejection.

Time clocks aside, let's now return to a couple's differing needs at night, and I'll begin with the man's side of the story.

Whether he is active or passive at work, a dynamo or "wet noodle," most men do deal with people and problems all day. So that when the husband comes home at night he's allergic to more people and more problems (especially his wife and *her* problems).

The husband feels that he's worked hard all day and has desperately tried to be a good provider. He thinks: Why isn't that enough? Why can't his wife appreciate him as he is? Didn't she used to respect his being a breadwinner? Wasn't that good enough at one point in their marriage? Now he comes home and never knows if he'll be greeted with open arms or a black Irish funk.

As Joseph Heller writes in his novel *Something Happened:*

I try my best to remember on what terms [my wife] and I parted this morning, or went to sleep last night, in order to know if she is still angry with

6

me for something I did or didn't say or do that I am no longer aware of. Is she mad or is she glad? I can't remember. And I am unable to tell. So I remain on guard. . . .

Consequently, the husband's evening routine begins with his being on guard, walking on eggshells. Thus, he becomes addicted to the evening news so that he won't have to talk. He hides behind the newspaper because he doesn't want to listen. He eats silently through dinner because he wants to avoid conflict at all costs. He can't stand one more demand. No more "Mr. Nice Guy." In fact, if he has to be nice to one more person, he'll go crazy. So he tunes out. Coming home is synonymous with tuning out.

Watching Monday night football or Tuesday night's movie, he's safe. No thinking is necessary. No decisions need be made. No responsibilities must be shouldered. At home he can finally relax.

Or can he?

Of course he can't.

Something has happened. The rules have changed. Whatever he does, it is never enough. Right or wrong, he is always wrong.

And so is his wife.

Here's a brief example. A woman consulted me because of an impending separation after seven years of marriage. She had decided that her husband had to put more time and energy into their marriage if it was to survive. There were to be no compromises. She had finally drawn the line. It was either her and the marriage, or a divorce. Period.

During a one-hour consultation in my office with her and her husband, the wife focused on a weekend problem. She said, "I want one day or even half a day for *us*. No more golf games on Sunday mornings, football games on Sunday afternoons, two-hour naps and silent dinners. I want one morning *or* afternoon every

7

Saturday *or* Sunday alone with you. Is that so unreasonable?"

At this point the following conversation ensued:

*The wife began:* I want some togetherness.

*He replied:* I want some space.

*Wife:* I need you to work on our relationship.

*Husband:* I work all week. I don't want to work on weekends. Why can't you understand that?!

*Wife:* I do understand. But we need some ground rules for Saturday and Sunday.

*Husband:* I hate ground rules. Can't we let the rules develop naturally?

*Wife:* They've developed so naturally I never see you anymore.

*Husband:* I need my freedom.

*Wife:* I need some closeness.

*Husband:* You're already so close it feels like there's a noose around my neck.

Here, the wife pressed her husband for another few minutes. She was desperate to get his attention. If she couldn't get it via direct communication, then she would get it via conflict. He, predictably, was desperately trying to avoid conflict. Quite naturally, he continued to resist her pressing him. So she continued to push. The conflict intensified. And suddenly, we had a classic example of a passive man fighting off a wild woman.

A few minutes later the wife lapsed into angry silence. She felt hurt, rejected and misunderstood. The husband felt misunderstood, too. Neither husband nor wife truly understood the other person's different needs, nor were they willing to accommodate for those differences. It was as if male and female were each speaking a different foreign language to each other without benefit of translation. Two trains passing in the night. Or more accurately, two trains on a collision course which ultimately ended in a wrecked marriage.

How typical is this story? I think it is extremely typical. I hear a variation on it in my office almost every week.

Frankly, problems about weekend plans are rarely solved with obvious and commonsense solutions. For example, it's unique to hear a passive husband say, actively and clearly: "Look, you're absolutely right. We should spend at least a day together on the weekends. But this Sunday San Francisco is playing Los Angeles, so what about our spending Saturday together. Is that O.K.?"

And it's equally rare to hear a wild wife say to her husband: "What's my role in the problem? What part am I playing in your aversion to time together? What changes are necessary in my behavior to create a better atmosphere at home?"

To say that I don't often hear such statements or questions is actually an understatement. Instead, the wife simply feels that her husband is more interested in television than he is in her. Whereas the husband feels that his wife hasn't a clue about his needs for privacy on Saturday and Sunday. He feels that if he gives an inch she'll take a mile. If he gives up a half day, she'll want the whole weekend.

And yet, the need for privacy is a very important point. For husband and wife, privacy is certainly as crucial in marriage as is communication. However, we frequently miss the boat about privacy in a good relationship. In fact, most of us end up feeling guilty for wanting a little time to ourselves.

But the reality is that some measure of privacy is absolutely crucial for any two people living under the same roof. Indeed, can any of us imagine a compatible relationship without it? Does not our survival as individuals depend upon our getting a daily supplement of quiet and solitude?

I heard one wife say that the bathroom was the only place in her house where she could hide and be left alone. It was the only room with a locked door. I heard about a husband who bought a mobile home and put it in his backyard. It was the only way he could escape from his family. A working couple said their only privacy came during the two-hour commute each took separately. Alone in their individual cars, they could finally roll up the windows and shut out the world. (And vent their domestic wrath on any car inadvertently crossing into their lane!)

The trouble is that bathrooms are uncomfortable and mobile homes are expensive. Cars are more usual, but only slightly better as vehicles for solving our problems of privacy.

The fact is that most husbands and wives need to relax alone at night. Especially if they've been active and responsible all day, they need time to be neither active nor responsible. They need a place to let down. And if a man cannot relax at home, where can he? At a bar? With male friends? A female friend? His secretary? Someone who understands him?

And if the woman cannot let down at home, where can she find peace and quiet? At night meetings? In evening classes? In her therapist's office? With her boss? With someone who understands her?

My point is a simple one. We need not only to talk in marriage, but we also need *not* to talk. We need a time and place to be alone.

The foregoing discussion about privacy has digressed somewhat from my original story. That is, the woman's need not only for privacy, but also for the man's participation in the home. So I would like now to return to the woman's side of a similar story. First of all, who are these women?

The wives I see for marital therapy don't easily fit

10

into any pigeonholes. They're of different ages and backgrounds. They defy stereotypes. Most hold full- or part-time jobs outside the home. Some are full-time homemakers. The majority have children, a few do not. They're women from twenty to sixty years of age. Most are middle class. A few are higher or lower on the economic ladder.

Except for those who are isolated all day, either in the house or on the job, almost every woman that I know also needs some privacy in her evening routine. Like her husband, she wants to relax at night. She too does not want extra demands or additional pressures after 7 or 8 o'clock at night. She also needs time alone. But there's a fundamental difference.

As I've said, working in the home or outside it, the woman I'm describing feels a crucial part of her day—the relationship—comes after her husband's arrival home. In addition to privacy, she needs to make direct contact. And she needs to connect with her husband, who often seems a million miles away, on an emotional level.

A wife's desire to tune in is as basic as is her husband's desire to tune out. Not surprisingly, these opposite needs set up a collision course.

Today we don't seem to recognize the basic differences or the collision course. Most women think they're crazy for wanting "something more" from a husband and marriage.

Of course, the husband agrees with her. She is crazy. Why else is his wife so terribly needy, the most dependent person in the world? Who else wants to have her cake, eat it too, and take home the silverware? So what else is new?

Most couples that I see in my office feel they have a unique problem. The wife wants too much and has become bitchy. The husband can't meet her needs. He ends up feeling guilty and sulky. And they both end up blaming each other.

11

Couples tell me over and over: "No one else seems to have our problems."

What can I say? "No one I see *doesn't* have your problems"?

These problems also extend into the bedroom. In fact, the reality of a passive husband is almost always compounded during sex. After all, sex is active. So a husband is expected during lovemaking to be actively tender, sensitive, expressive, aggressive, regressive, loving, passionate, spontaneous, rested, and when ready— let loose, go wild and be a little crazy. All of this is supposed to come from a man who is passive out of bed and who may be in touch with his feelings only via satellite. Lovemaking is probably the most sensitive thermostat of a man's ability to be emotionally active in a relationship. No wonder things break down after several years of marriage, especially in the bedroom.

However, the different sexual needs of men and women at night are often manifested in totally different ways. For instance:

A man can be angry, annoyed, irritated or out-to-lunch at home. And yet, he can come to bed and want a "quickie" with his wife. The fact that he has hardly spoken to her in fourteen hours (or days) doesn't really affect his libido.

Most women are different. Before intercourse a wife wants to feel connected to her husband so that she can relax and enjoy good sex. Frozen out of the relationship for hours or days, she wants to resolve hostilities and close emotional distances between them. A little warmth from her husband goes a long way toward good lovemaking.

However, these sexual expectations and differences are not always clear. They pop up in bed in strange ways.

Take, for example, an evening when a wife sends out clear sexual signals from the moment her husband comes home. She has done her hair, put on makeup, changed into something "comfortable." Maybe there's a candlelight dinner or a favorite wine awaiting his arrival. Maybe there's a direct statement: "Let's go to bed early tonight and not watch TV."

The husband may or may not decipher his wife's message. I don't think it really matters. What does matter is the husband's response. He still comes home and wants to tune out. In spite of his wife's attempted seduction, he still wants to hide behind the evening paper and watch Monday night football.

Maybe his wife's impending seduction even adds to his anxieties. He experiences the upcoming sex not only as a pressure, but as a HUGE pressure. After all, he must eventually obtain and maintain an erection. He must perform in bed. And in the face of that pressure, real or imagined, a husband may suddenly become desperate to watch every bit of that Monday night football game in spite of the score being 35 to 0 in the last quarter.

Meanwhile, the wife senses her husband's allergic reaction to her. Consequently, when he finally does come to bed, her needs for closeness are even greater. (Unless, of course, she's given up and gone to sleep.) Thus, assuming she still wants to make love, the wife continues trying to make emotional contact after the lights are out.

She says, "Talk to me. Who won the game? Tell me what you're thinking. How did your day go? Did I tell you about what happened to me downtown when I ran into . . ."

Unfortunately, his wife's need to talk comes as an added pressure for the husband. He would willingly make love (he thinks) if only she'd keep quiet. He'd enjoy sex if she didn't go on and on. Words, words, words, words!

*He thinks:*   If only she'd shut up.
*She thinks:*   If only he'd talk to me.

| She says: | Who won? |
|---|---|
| He says: | It doesn't matter. |
| She says: | How did the day go? |
| He says: | Don't ask. |
| She says: | What are you thinking about? |
| He says: | Nothing. |
| She says: | Did I tell you about . . . |
| He says: | Tell me tomorrow. |

Ultimately, she turns off. He rolls over. She feels unloved. He may not have the foggiest idea what just happened and promptly falls asleep.

Sexual and nonsexual differences often get obscured in marriage. Each partner feels repeatedly rejected. She ends up feeling confused, hurt, furious and frustrated. He ends up feeling pushed, pressured, inadequate and guilty.

My point is a simple one: All this couple has heard is that they should communicate, but no one has told them how to achieve that communication. Nor has anyone said that a lot of men and women have different needs at night. The wife does not realize that difference as she takes Excedrin for headaches, nor does the man realize it as he takes Gelusil for his heartburn. Neither recognizes the difference as they swallow Valium for their anxiety.

Because I think it is such an obvious secret, let me translate the difference into simple declarative sentences. I would say to the couples who recognize themselves in this kind of marriage and want to unite: "Remember! You're two different animals. Men and women cannot totally unite. Most husbands and wives have needs at night which are 180 degrees opposite each other's. It's true of 95 percent of married couples I know. You are *not* alone."

Of course a lot of husbands and wives do feel alone. Sadly, they do not understand these basic differences between them. Core problems are never defined. Re-

14

alities are not confronted. Accommodations are not made. With the result: No lasting solutions are ever achieved and the collision course repeats itself over and over and over. Meanwhile our divorce rate continues to go up and up and up.

•

*To be a woman is a great adventure;*
*To drive men mad is a heroic thing.*

Boris Pasternak
Doctor Zhivago

What else is going on here? What other factors contribute to this phenomenon of male passivity, at least at home?

The popular reason given today is the women's movement. Women's liberation. Feminine demands for equal rights and equal orgasms. The new pressures on men— new to the past decade.

Maybe that's part of the story. I think it is. But it is only a small part. I think the reasons for the problem are actually historical. Its roots lie much deeper. And it is our understanding of that history and those roots that is absolutely crucial to our ultimately solving the dilemma.

So let us ask: How long have differences between husband and wife existed? Hasn't the most important part of many a woman's day always been her relationships at home? Haven't most men always felt it was more crucial to work and make a living?

To answer these questions, here is a summary of some fascinating findings by Dr. David Gutmann, Chief of Psychology at Northwestern University Medical School, who extensively studied traditional male and female roles in three cultures: Mayan Indians, American Indians, and Middle East peasants. In these three groups, and in many other cultures throughout the world, a consistent male and female role has been found in the early years of marriage.

To be more specific, there occurs in a couple's twenties what is called an "emergency of parenthood." During this emergency of child rearing the husband is assertive. As a young father he spends his time providing food, shelter and security for his family. Survival depends upon him.

While providing for his family, the man gives up another side of himself, commonly called his dependency needs: qualities like nurturing, tenderness, receptivity and passivity. He does so because these so-called feminine needs might interfere with the courage required to protect and provide for the physical security of his family.

Meanwhile, his wife also gives up a side of herself during the emergency of parenthood. She gives up a more assertive, masculine side which could both alienate her husband and interfere with the raising of her children. During the early years of child rearing she tends to remain passive, receptive, accepting and dependent.

As they grow up, the children understandably begin to take over the responsibility of their own security. The emergency of protecting and raising a family slowly passes for the parents and, as the need for security passes, an important *role reversal* occurs in the middle years.

What is that reversal?

Men begin to live out their passivity which was earlier repressed for the sake of defense. The warrior's armor is no longer needed. Hence, the man may slowly become more interested in religion, art and aesthetics. A certain softness, even tenderness, may emerge. Finally, by middle age, he may begin to relax.

It has also been found across a wide range of societies that most wives repossess their more assertive side in middle life. After their child-rearing years they become less dependent and more independent. As Dr. Gutmann notes, "Grandma becomes more decisive, tough-minded and intrusive. Grandpa becomes sweeter, more affable but rather vague."

Or to put it into the words of an old Moroccan parable:

Each man is born surrounded by a hundred devils; each woman by a hundred angels. However, with each passing year, a devil is exchanged for an angel. So, by one hundred years of age the man is surrounded entirely by angels. And the woman is surrounded entirely by devils.

Today I think those Moroccan angels and devils are being exchanged between husband and wife at a somewhat earlier stage. Long before he becomes a grandfather, a man is likely to become affable, passive and rather vague. Whereas at a much earlier age than did her grandmother, his wife may become more decisive and tough-minded.

Why?

Because male and female roles have radically changed over the last hundred years. The role reversal that I've described has accelerated due to changes in both men and women. We'll look at each in turn.

Before the Industrial Revolution a man had to assert his physical strength. He had to hunt, fish, fight or farm in order to provide for his family. His strength served not only a vital function, but it offered the man an important psychological defense. A man's greater muscular strength defended him against a woman's greater emotional strength.

Throughout history, I think, a majority of men have feared being unmanly. More specifically, I believe they have feared women. Myth and religion both speak in great detail about these fears of men in relation to

17

women. Man's fear of a woman's inherent power is most frequently expressed as distrust. You have only to look at a few proverbs from around the world to see that this has been voiced in almost every culture:

Never believe a woman, not even a dead one.
*An old German proverb*

A woman's tongue is only three inches long, but it can kill a man six feet high.
*Japanese proverb*

Woman is a calamity but every house must have its curse.
*Persian proverb*

Do not trust a good woman, and keep away from a bad one.
*Portuguese proverb*

Three things are useless: whispering to the deaf, grieving for the dead, and advising a woman against her will.
*Welsh proverb*

Current misconceptions to the contrary, men have clearly been afraid of women for centuries. Husbands intuitively knew their wives were better in relationships and could dominate and destroy them if they got too close. Small wonder that, historically, men have felt they had to defend themselves against this fear of women.

For example, almost 2,500 years ago, the Greek male's contempt for women was bound to his extreme fear of them. Why else would such Greek customs be necessary as a wife's not being older than her husband or of higher social status? Customs such as a woman's not being paid the same as a male for the same work; customs not allowing women to be in a position of authority. All of these social conventions reveal that

Greek males were really afraid of competing with females on an equal basis.

The deck of cards had to be stacked and the man given an advantage. Otherwise the Greeks thought the man would be consumed, overwhelmed and lose his tenuous identity.

Before machines, a man could not only stack the deck but use his greater physical strength as a defense. As I've said, male strength was needed for production and protection and survival. But the Industrial Revolution changed a man's role forever. Industrialization diminished the importance of physical strength. Modern machines could work equally for both sexes. Consequently, a man's strength was not only minimized but, in the process, he was robbed of a vital psychological defense. He became even more susceptible to a woman's emotional powers.

Over the past one hundred years I think man has become like a turtle without a shell. In relation to a woman, he feels unprotected, exposed and vulnerable. Understandably he desperately clings to the old notion: Be a good provider and your wife will be happy.

The kicker is, of course, that his wife isn't happy. And not only is his wife unhappy and dissatisfied, but she has become more assertive about her dissatisfaction. She has accelerated that middle-age role reversal. She has become infinitely more independent at a much earlier age than was her grandmother.

Why?

The role reversal for women has been accelerated recently by many factors, but three stand out:

1. *Birth control.* Most of us have forgotten that an average family of two hundred years ago had eight children. Today an average family has less than two children. In fact, one out of four college-educated wives in the United States has no children at all. With modern contraception a woman now has a choice about her family. She can choose to have a few or no children.

Hence, a couple's "emergency of parenthood" is either condensed into a shorter time span or, if they have no children, of course there is simply no such emergency at all.

The result is that a woman today has infinitely more freedom of choice than did her grandmother. With fewer or no children, a woman's tremendous energies are freed to be expressed in other ways.

2. *Our divorce rate.* Let's review briefly some staggering statistics about divorce in America. In 1890 there were 570,000 marriages and 33,461 divorces in the United States, a ratio of 17 marriages to 1 divorce. Today, almost a hundred years later, there are annually about 2 million marriages and 1 million divorces, a ratio approaching 2 to 1.

I will speak at length in Part III about how and why the traditional expectation for a woman to "live through her husband to be happy" is no longer working for most women. Suffice it to say, however, a majority of women today can count on less than the fingers of one hand the number of truly happily married women they know. Consequently, many women are increasingly independent, not only in search of their own identity, but also because they have seen too many divorced friends. These are friends who were once almost totally dependent in their marriage. And, following a divorce, they are left ill-prepared and ill-equipped to deal with the economic and psychological realities of life on their own. The price of total dependency has been high. In retrospect, the need to develop a more independent side seems clear both to them and their friends.

3. *Jobs for women:* Given this picture, it is really not surprising that we have seen a tremendous influx of women into the job market. This influx has occurred because of economic necessity as well as a search for an independent identity. It has also occurred because more women are having fewer or no children. What-

ever the reasons, the increase in working women over the past thirty years is one of the most significant social changes of our time.

Over the last three decades the number of working wives in America increased by 205 percent, and today a majority of mothers with school-age children—six to seventeen years—hold jobs outside the home. In fact, a majority of all adult women in this country are now in the labor market. It is the first time in history. That fact alone has dramatically altered traditional male and female roles.

Man is obviously no longer the sole provider of food, shelter and physical protection. He has been stripped of his centuries-old function.

Nor is his wife bound by pregnancy after pregnancy to a life over which she has little or no apparent control. She has infinitely more freedom at a much earlier age than had her grandmother. And yet, she has also been stripped of her basic and traditional role.

In short, male and female roles are in a state of rapid flux today. Each partner stands relatively naked before the other. Their past is gone and their future is unclear. The result is to raise mutual anxieties. Passive men withdraw under those anxieties. Wild women attack. And both end up taking it out on each other.

•

*Inflation has become so rampant that I've heard America's supermarkets described as the churches of today. You walk down the aisle and hear everybody saying, "Oh my God. Oh my God!"*

Ann Landers

Wherever I've spoken about the need for men to be more active at home I am inevitably asked, "But what about our high inflation rate? What about our staggering cost of living? Don't most men *and* women have to work and make a living? Don't they deserve to be passive at home?"

The answer, of course, is yes. Most of us do have to make a living. Indeed we work incredibly hard at it. As one small example of just how hard we work, let's take the cost of raising a family. It used to be that children were a great financial asset to a family. Today they are a tremendous economic liability. It used to be that adolescents worked to help support a family. But today the reverse is true.

One set of recent figures estimates that it costs an American middle-class family $60,000 to $80,000 to support a child. A high-income family, whose child may receive private school education all the way, is going to have to pay nearer $150,000. For a lower-income family the figure is $30,000. There's no doubt these costs will get worse. And it is not only because of inflation.

Historically, schooling has increased as the amount of work has decreased. During the Depression, for example, school was extended to the eleventh and twelfth grades in America. This was not entirely for altruistic or educational purposes. On the contrary, it was because few jobs were available in the United States during the 1930s. Consequently, a child's stay in school was lengthened to eliminate adolescents from entering the job market. With that change, adolescence in America was extended and a family's expenditures on their children were prolonged.

Meanwhile, the rising cost of education (and everything) continues unabated today. Therefore, most of us not only work extremely hard, but we also have to spend hard. Our spending, in turn, can lead to a self-defeating cycle: Earn > spend > earn more > work more > spend more. Consequently, regardless of the fact that both husband and wife may hold jobs, there's seldom enough of either time or money. After taxes, expenditures always seem to exceed income.

Thus, most of us are constantly exceeding our income and are forever floored. We are floored by our inflation rate and rising cost of everything. We are floored by our charge accounts, bank balances, credit cards, and fly now/pay later way of life. We are also floored by the daily rat race. After all, if we aren't at our desk the full working day or even longer, how can we pay the bills and get ahead? Consequently, most of us keep our nose pressed firmly to the grindstone lest our debts spin wildly out of control.

So, again, the answer is yes. We do expend an incredible amount of energy to earn a living. And yes, both partners definitely deserve to come home and be passive after work. Or more accurately, both husbands and wives deserve a large measure of individual privacy in their own home.

At this point, however, I would like to look beyond our high cost of living (and high cost of *making* a living). I want to suggest that our home life is equally affected by another, absolutely fundamental reality about our work life.

Put simply, it is the reality that most of us wear a mask on our jobs. We put our best face forward. Whether we are male or female, active or passive, tigers or mice at the office—one of our biggest jobs on the job is to get along with other people. Consequently, from nine to five, or whatever our hours, we laugh a lot and don't make waves. We walk around with a cheerful face. We grin and bear it.

The fact is that work is not the appropriate place to show our true feelings. The rewards for such honesty are few. Therefore, in spite of an occasional and overwhelming urge to swing from the chandeliers and shout obscenities at everyone, we don't. Instead, we just smile and look sincere.

This external and internal world at work is contrasted with painful accuracy once again by Joseph Heller in *Something Happened*. The main character in the book, Bob Slocum, considers showing his true feelings at work, albeit passively, and wonders what would happen if he ever bucked the system:

> What would happen, I speculate gloomily every two weeks or so as I tear open the blank, buff pay envelope . . . if I did spindle, fold, tear, deface, staple, and mutilate it? (It's my paycheck, isn't it? Or is it?) What would happen if, deliberately, calmly, with malice aforethought and obvious premeditation, I disobeyed?
>
> I know what would happen: nothing. Nothing would happen. And the knowledge depresses me.

So Bob Slocum, like most of us, automatically continues to keep the lid on at work. He continues to seek approval and avoid rebellion. He does so because he knows it would do no good.

> My act of rebellion would be absorbed like rain on an ocean and leave no trace. It would not cause a ripple.
>
> I suppose it is just about impossible for someone like me to rebel anymore and produce any kind of lasting effect . . . They would simply fire and forget me as soon as I tried. They would file me away.

Most of us too would be fired, forgotten and filed away if we ever showed our true feelings at work. It is nearly impossible, in spite of those irresistible impulses, for us to spindle, fold or mutilate anything (or anybody) on the job. Consequently, during the day most of us wear a respectable mask and, through it, we eat an enormous amount of humble pie.

If there is one feeling common to almost every job, it is frustration. And yet, how many work situations allow their employees the luxury of expressing their frustrations, let alone their anger? If there is one emotion forbidden to express on almost every job, it is, I think, our anger.

I hear this reality repeatedly from both men and women in my office. From corporate executives to factory workers, there's no being honest on most jobs. There's simply no way in the world to express negative (angry) feelings at work. As I say, the rewards for such honesty are nil. Therefore daily anger, like the daily garbage, piles up within most of us because we have so little chance to dump it.

I admit there are a few exceptions to the rule. For example, there are several trial lawyers I know who can kill (with words) on cross examination in a courtroom; a few surgeons who routinely shout and throw their surgical instruments in the midst of an operation; wheeler-dealer types who can destroy their competition (and clients) in business deals. And, of course, there are professional athletes who are paid enormous sums to wipe out the opposition.

However, litigating lawyers, screaming surgeons and competitive superstars probably account for less than one-tenth of 1 percent of the working population. Most of us, like Bob Slocum, must keep our killer instincts to ourselves. We must store up our daily frustrations to the point where our reservoir is overflowing. So in spite of our smiling face and sincere looks, we really carry an enormous load on our shoulders (or in our stomachs). As Bob Slocum says:

I've got eight unhappy people working for me who have problems and unhappy dependents of their own. I've got anxiety; I suppress hysteria. I've got politics on my mind, summer race riots, drugs, violence and teen-age sex. There are perverts and deviates everywhere who might corrupt or strangle any one of my children. I've got crime in my streets. I've got old

25

age to face. My boy, though only nine, is already worried because he does not know what he wants to be when he grows up. My daughter tells lies. I've got the decline of American civilization and the guilt and ineptitude of the whole government of the United States to carry around on these poor shoulders of mine.

And I find I am being groomed for a better job. And I find—God help me—that I want it.

Not only is it Bob Slocum who wants that better job. It is most of us. We want it because, at a fundamental level, we must pay the bills and, regardless of our staggering cost of living, we desperately want a better life for ourselves and our family.

And yet, there is another reason for our wanting to get ahead on the job. It is a more profound reason and is a variation on the theme of male and female roles being in a state of rapid flux today.

Our job gives most of us a clear role. It does so at a time, as I've stressed, when male and female roles are unclear. Although we may feel relatively lost at home, we know who we are and what to do at work. Our job infuses meaning and purpose into our lives. It offers a direction to our day. It provides us with an identity, however tenuous.

Work can also offer the approval and applause often so lacking elsewhere in our lives. On the job there is usually at least someone (or several people) who appreciate our work. And, God knows, most of us need all the approval, applause and appreciation we can get.

The trouble is that our getting approval at work may also be a self-defeating cycle. It can reinforce our tendency to keep the lid on our true feelings. After all, if we ever showed our honest emotions on the job how would we get approval? How would we get those rewards? Who would like us? Therefore, our keeping the lid on negative feelings becomes not only a logical way to get ahead, it also becomes a way of life.

The problem is that keeping the lid on our feelings in search of approval is not only a full-time job, it is also exhausting. We are forever onstage with other people, always wearing that false mask with a fixed smile.

The other problem with being onstage is that we must play to an ever-changing audience. And unfortunately, today's audience may want something new tomorrow. Approval is elusive. People are fickle. Rules change. Applause can turn to silence. Silence to indifference. So we keep doing our dance lest our audience become bored and lose interest in us.

So what happens when we come offstage? What happens when we come home at night?

Whereas it is true that our ability to get approval may be one reason for our success on the job, it is also true that our wearing a mask (assuming we don't take it off) compounds our problems at home. It doesn't make the expression of true feelings any easier.

But here's another difference between most men and women. It is usually easier for the woman to take off her mask and make the transition at night from being a work person to a home person.

For example, I have a patient who is an extremely successful advertising executive in San Francisco. As she succinctly put it:

"My hours are from eight in the morning until eight in the evening, sometimes without a break. Also, when I get home, I know I have another hour or two of work ahead of me. However, I usually need a glass of wine and a warm bath or half-hour of TV (half-hour is tops!) to make that transformation from a work person into a home person. But that's all it takes. After a half-hour, I am anxious to talk with my husband. And if he won't talk to me, which is rather typical, I am anxious to talk with anyone who wants to share life's experiences. That usually means my women friends."

The husband's not talking with his wife *is* rather typical. Indeed, most men I know have infinitely greater difficulty making this same transition from being a work person to home person, taking off their mask, and sharing life experiences on an intimate level.

Why? Because most men are ill-prepared and ill-equipped to share their innermost feelings at night. To be emotionally active in a relationship is extremely hard. Hard because it implies (and involves) more work for which most men have had little or no preparation.

The average husband, passive or not, comes to his private life almost totally untrained to deal with the realities of an intimate relationship. He has not learned how to be an active participant at home from his own father. He has not learned from his mother. (This lack of an apprenticeship will be the subject of Part II.) And he has certainly not learned on most jobs, where his wearing of a mask only compounds the basic problem.

Given this lack of preparation, is it really a wonder that many a man drives home the long way and, once he hits the front door, just wants to withdraw, relax, unwind, be quiet and left alone?

It's very difficult for almost every man I know—as his wife pleads, "Just talk to me, tell me what you're feeling." (Damn it!)—to suddenly start expressing something he may not even be aware of. On automatic pilot all day, how does he know what he's feeling at night?

Or more honestly, he does know what he's feeling. He's feeling angry. Annoyed. Resentful. Furious. He feels nailed to the wall, pressured and trapped. It is as if his wife suddenly turned to him and said, "I love you." Cornered, he feels as if a loaded gun has just been pointed at his head. And, with a loaded pistol aimed at his head, what can a man say except, "I love you, *too*."

In addition, the man feels like he's been going 90 m.p.h. all day. Suddenly he's expected to slow down and shift gears at night. He's expected to take off his mask. He is expected to work "on the relationship." He is told to tune in to his feelings. Express himself. Raise his consciousness. Say what he is thinking and feeling. Be honest.

Be honest?

In theory, that sounds terrific. After all, what is the purpose of marriage? Is not one purpose to provide at least one place in the world to take off our mask? But, in reality, for men and women alike, where can we be honest? Where can we be honestly cranky? Where can we honestly let down and be irritable? Where can we honestly explode? Who can we kick? Where can we take off the mask, dump the daily garbage, and spill our overflowing reservoir of daily misadventures?

If the husband were really honest, his wife would think, "Oh God, here we go again." "Grow up." "Don't whine." "All you do is complain." Or "Why do you always have to kick ME?" Just as he thinks when his wife lets out her frustrations, "Why does she always have to be so unhappy, so hysterical, all the time?"

The paradox is obvious. What most of us really want, I think, is not a totally honest expression of feelings, but rather a limited kind of honesty from the other person. What we'd truly like is for our husband or wife to be honestly calm. Honestly charming. Honestly cheerful, diplomatic and reasonable. Honestly interesting and interested in us. In short, we'd like them to be at night just as they've been all day with other people. BE NICE!

*Men become older, but they never become good.*
                                        Oscar Wilde

The broad brush picture I am painting is one of a husband and wife on a collision course due to their differing needs at night. Unrecognized, and in the extreme, these differences can lead not only to a self-destructive marriage but to an eventual divorce. Let's now look at what happens today to many men and women hit by this epidemic of marital failure.

To start with the ex-husband after a divorce, how does he find a woman who will simply accept him as a good provider? Are there females who will allow him to be active at work and passive at home? Where does he discover a woman who will offer some applause, provide a personal rooting section for his achievements? Where does he find a woman who will not be jealous of his intrinsic wish to remain independent and mobile within a new marriage?

In my office I hear repeatedly about thirty-, forty-, and fifty-year-old men who leave an old marriage and usually follow two predictable paths. Initially these men enjoy a series of one-night stands. They pick up women in singles' bars and avoid any serious involvement. Like a dog who has been chained up for days or weeks, the ex-husband suddenly breaks his chains and his first reaction is to run around the block like a crazy man, leaving his mark everywhere.

More profoundly, after his new-found freedom, the same man often follows a second pathway. This path leads him to be attracted to inordinately young women. He is unconsciously attracted to younger females and it is with such a woman that he finally settles down.

Why?

The popular explanation is that the male ego is shattered in a destructive marriage. Sexually, the man must prove himself after a divorce. He needs to restore his confidence and build his self-esteem. Not surprisingly, most people say that the older man picks a younger woman to prove himself and his masculinity, especially in bed.

This may be part of the story; however, it is only a small part. The real attraction of older men to younger women, I believe, has very little to do with sex. The attraction of an autumn/spring relationship has more to do with a man's desire to find a woman who will accept him as he is. He seeks a woman who will confirm his individual value. He looks for someone who will admire and adore him. A woman who will provide that personal rooting section for his uniqueness and accomplishments.

The man chooses a younger woman because she will respect his breadwinning talents (which are often greater as he gets older) and appreciate those talents. She will admire him just as his wife was once admiring of him. And because of that admiration she will water and fertilize and care for his every need. In short, he views the younger woman as less of a threat.

This is not a new story. To draw a parallel with early Greece: In the Greek tragedies, it is the young women and virginal goddesses who are helpful to men. Meanwhile, the mature goddesses tend to be portrayed as jealous, vindictive and destructive. Indeed in the daily life of Athens during the fifth century B.C., there was a tendency for males to marry barely pubescent girls.

So too, the once disappointed modern man is likely to choose a younger woman the next time around largely because he feels there will be no more demands to talk endlessly into the night. On the contrary. He has images of coming home to his slippers and pipe,

31

a crackling fire and a quiet evening. At last he can have some privacy in his own house.

Is it a wonder the ex-husband views a younger woman as absolute bliss? After all those years of marital warfare the man feels he has discovered peace at last. Paradise found!

But does it last? Ultimately, does not the new wife, too, begin to ask for "something more"? Like any woman worth her salt, does she not also want an emotional connection with her man?

After several years of marriage, is it enough for a woman today to make a full-time job out of confirming her man's independence and individual worth? Is it enough for her to be a silent witness to his public achievements? I think it is not enough. Like his former wife, the new woman also wants her husband to come close and be active in their relationship.

Let's now turn to the husband's former wife and ask what happens to her after the breakup of a marriage.

It is usually hard and bewildering for her to watch an aging ex-husband choose a younger woman. It is especially hard knowing how much more she has to offer a man who would appreciate *her* talents.

I recently read an interview with an anonymous author in the New York *Times*. She was described only as "a moderately famous writer of a certain age." In the interview the author looks at autumn/spring romances and her own advancing years. From a woman's perspective she summarizes the problem:

I used to attract men because I looked sexy. Now I look intelligent and it turns them off. To understand a man is considered a form of aggression. When they gaze into my eyes, they see the truth. I'm like a shaving mirror. What am I supposed to do—play dumb? I've seen everything twice, or three times, and I'm glad I did. Most men chase young women, but what is a young woman? A *tabula rasa,* a blank page. To go around with a young woman is like wanting to write a novel and being afraid to start it. To be with me is like reading one.

I will describe in detail what happens to a majority of such women who are looking for interesting and available men following a divorce. However, before doing so, I want to look at what occurs to an increasing minority of women after their marriage breaks up.

To be more specific, I am currently hearing in my office about women who are left or leave their marriage and they, like their ex-husband, begin looking for a younger mate. Although their search may be the exception rather than the rule, I think these women's spring attractions are significant and worth brief mention.

For example, that "moderately famous writer of a certain age" also said:

Some women my age amuse themselves with boys, the kind of boys who look like they're sold in drugstores. At one time, an older woman could attract an interesting young man with her style. But only gay types understand style these days. When anyone under thirty starts coming on with me, he's usually looking for a mother, and you know what's happened to mothers.

Maybe younger men are looking for older mother figures. Some obviously are. But from a woman's point of view the attraction to a younger man, I think, is due to a different reason.

She wants a man who has some energy to match her own. Unlike her tired but successful middle-aged husband, the younger man is not chronically exhausted at night. Sexually and nonsexually, a man five or fifteen years younger than these women often provides what their husbands could not. Energy and interest. Passion and hormones.

However, there's another important aspect to the story of women who do attract younger men. A majority of these women tell me that in spite of the new energy and intensity put into their relationship, passion is not the total answer.

One divorced designer said that she enjoyed good sex for the first time in years with a younger lover. He was tender, kind, sensitive to her every need. He was totally devoted to her.

But, fortunately or unfortunately, the young man didn't hold a job; or more accurately, his work was sporadic and halfhearted. After six months the woman confessed, "I really don't like making more money than he does. Perhaps I'm old-fashioned. But I prefer the man to earn more than I do. And I certainly don't want to support him for any lengthy period of time. That's why I could never marry him."

Another divorced woman in her late forties was attracted to a man in his mid-twenties. He too did not work. In fact, his major effort in life was to devote himself entirely to his woman and their relationship. He picked her up at work, cleaned house, made dinner and made love.

At first, the older woman devoured the young man's attention. For months she couldn't get enough of it. She was starved for the affection. And yet, again, something happened. The intensity of the man's twenty-four-hour-a-day devotion began to smother her. She felt suffocated by the relationship. She needed a breather. She, like her previous husband, suddenly needed some distance and privacy from the person she was supporting. After being starved for affection in her marriage, she was now being overwhelmed with it in the new relationship and ultimately, she left the young man. She went off to seek a middle ground, if one existed.

For older and younger women alike, I think it is extremely difficult to find that middle ground after a divorce. Indeed, even if a woman looks for someone her own age or older, she quickly discovers the truth of that simple refrain: A good man is hard to find.

A good man *is* difficult to find as well as hold, and nowhere is that really better illustrated than in the example of what happens to another group of ex-wives. These are the majority of women that I see in my office after their marriage breaks up.

I said that it was common for men after a divorce to look for a younger woman. What is common for their ex-wives is to seek a man of any reasonable age who is willing to invest some energy into his personal life.

But what happens?

Increasingly, the answer I hear is a variation on the theme of male passivity. It is an answer which is coming with more and more frequency from divorced men as well as women. However, the bottom line is almost always the same. Available men are wary of making a commitment. Instead, they prefer to engage in a long (or short) relationship with a long (or short) series of women. Why?

From the divorced man's point of view, he may be wary because of the high cost, economically and emotionally, of a previous marriage. He is wary because he was burned once and doesn't want to be burned again. He's reluctant to vow "for richer or poorer" because it is he who will end up poorer. He feels that "till death do us part" means that yet another woman is going to try to kill him.

From the woman's side, especially after going with the same man for several months or years, the story is different. She does want a commitment. And yet such a woman also knows her man at an intuitive level. She realizes that he is as allergic to commitment as is a married man to closeness.

This allergy, however, may or may not be apparent

during the beginning of such a relationship. Every-thing can go fine during the initial days, weeks or months of a new romance. Energy is high, talk is easy, sex is good. But again, something happens.

Overtly and covertly, the woman starts to convey a desire for "something more" from the man. For exam-ple, she wants more frequent sex or a more honest expression of his feelings or more time together. Of course the man is ultrasensitive to her desires (which he reacts to as demands) and he immediately feels the pressure. If the woman pushes slightly, he backs off abruptly.

Rather than become hysterical, I have found that most unmarried women also will back off. This is not only a defense to protect themselves against rejection, but it is also because the women don't want to seem too pushy.

To give a more elaborate example, I have a friend who is a part-time photographer. She's a divorced woman in her mid-thirties with two small daughters. I think that my friend is an attractive person in every way. Not only does she have good looks but she also has an abundance of common sense. She's an extreme-ly kind person with a good heart and unlimited potential.

My friend is also clear about her needs as a woman. She wants a man who will be actively involved with her at home. She, too, wants "something more" and she has had an absolute devil of a time finding a good man.

Her story is not atypical.

Shortly after her divorce my friend became involved with a man who had a classic allergy to commitment. He was a recently separated lawyer in his early forties, and he bounced like a Ping-Pong ball between my friend and his ex-wife. One weekend he made love to my friend. The next weekend he disappeared. Two days would be spent with my friend; two days with his ex-wife.

On vacations it was the same story. One week with my friend in New Mexico; a week with "his other woman" in Canada. He went up and down like a yo-yo and so did the two women on his string.

After a year my friend agreed with my diagnosis. Her boyfriend was allergic to making a commitment. He kept breaking out in rashes of indecision. Whenever he entered the pollen field of a relationship, he broke out in emotional hives. He was so ambivalent, in fact, that every time either his wife or mistress got too close he fled in a panic. His wife thought he was weak. My friend called him wishy-washy. Both felt he was too damn passive.

The paradox was that the lawyer wanted to make a commitment, but he couldn't. He was unable to give either woman that "something more." Consequently, he ended up feeling not only inadequate but guilty.

The lawyer wasn't a malicious person. Nor did he have a particular need to hurt either woman. He was simply allergic to closeness with his wife in the old marriage. And now he was equally allergic to making a commitment with my friend in a new marriage. He was immobilized.

And yet the lawyer had his side of the story. From his perspective, whenever he gave "something more" to his wife or my friend (a little talk, an honest expression of his feelings or good sex) he felt it only whetted their appetites. It was just an appetizer. He perceived my friend and his ex-wife as voracious. His appetizers only made them hungrier. They seemed insatiable. They wanted more and MORE!

The question in his mind was, could he fill their needs? Could he ever satisfy either woman?

It was a familiar problem. The man wanted freedom and mobility in the relationship, while both women needed some sense of fusion. Unfortunately, neither my friend nor the man's wife defined these differences, nor did they act on them. It took two years before my friend finally gave up on the lawyer and his inability to make a commitment.

It saddens me to have to conclude this story by pointing out that my friend ended up feeling empty, unloved, inadequate and overwhelmingly depressed by having experienced the whole affair. She was also angry and yet, underneath her anger, my friend knew that she had lost something very important during the relationship. She had lost a part of herself and her own identity. She had lost no small amount of time in a two-year affair with an uncommitted man. Just as she had lost a lot of her youth during a twelve-year marriage with a distressingly passive husband. Even if these losses varied in intensity, they led just as devastatingly to the woman's feeling hopeless and pessimistic about her future with any man.

Current clichés aside, I do not think that my friend today views men as too strong, too powerful, too involved, too active *in their relationships*. On the contrary, she sees most men as too weak, immature, ineffectual, indifferent, uninvolved, inactive, uncaring, apathetic, absent and out-to-lunch *at home*.

Consequently, for my friend as well as women like her, I think some of the basic questions are: Is it true that a good man is hard to find? And if so, where does a woman find one? How does she find a man who will make a meaningful commitment; a man who will come close and still play an active role at home? Where is the man who will appreciate *her* talents? In short, where can she discover a man with whom to intermingle feelings, combat loneliness, and share a life together?

Frankly, I think it's hard for a woman.

# PART II

---

## More About Men

•

*Honor thy father and thy mother.*

*Exodus*

Why is it so hard for a man to come close and play an active role at home? Why is it so difficult for him to take off his mask and express a wide variety of his innermost feelings?

Earlier I said that most men come to marriage ill-prepared to deal with the demands of an intimate life. In general, they do not learn from their fathers how to be active men in their own homes.

To elaborate, I now want to turn to why men are passive in terms of *models* that men have had over the years. Models for fathers. Models for mothers. And how these models have contributed to our current epidemic of passive men.

Historically, before the Industrial Revolution, we were primarily a rural economy. Over 50 percent of the population lived on farms, and anyone who grew up on a farm knows that one's father was around. True, he may have left the house at five in the morning. But he came back for breakfast. He went out again, yet he returned for a mid-morning break or lunch. He usually came home for dinner and the evening.

A hundred years ago school may have been part of a child's day. However, an apprenticeship under one's father was the most important, richest part of a boy's life growing up. He worked with his father. And, whereas there may have been problems between the two men, sons at least were in intimate contact with their dads.

Also, there was often similar contact with two or three generations of men: uncles, cousins, grandparents and maybe even great-grandparents who, if they didn't actually live in the same house, lived on nearby farms. This extended family offered the boy a broad range in age and style of male models to choose from.

With the Industrial Revolution, life changed. There was mass migration into the cities and factories. Immigration from Western and Eastern Europe increased in earnest to provide much of the labor force for the new industrialized society.

Consequently, by the turn of the century, there was a fundamental change in most American families. Urban fathers still left home early, but they were quite likely not to come back until late at night. *Absent fathers became the rule.* And grandfathers, by the mid-twentieth century, were shunted off to retirement villages or old persons' homes.

It is true that in the 1920s and 1930s some men began escaping the factories and sweatshops. (People like my own father entered professions, others started businesses.) But most of our fathers still worked eight to twelve hours a day hoping to give us, their children, something they had not fully achieved: a sense of security, a better education, material possessions . . . the list went on. The result, however, did not change. Our fathers remained essentially *absent* from home.

Personally, although I had great respect for my father, I never really knew him in any depth. Nor have most of my patients, male and female, truly known their fathers. He was simply a hard-working man who left early in the morning and came back extremely tired at night. Like many of the husbands I've described, our fathers, too, came home to have a few drinks, hide behind a newspaper, eat silently through dinner, retreat to the living room and collapse on the couch.

Variations on the absent father included a man who, although home, was out of touch with his children. He expected them to be seen and not heard. It was the mother who was close to the children. The father always seemed something of an outsider. He too was no more a positive model for his son than if he were absent.

D. H. Lawrence eloquently captures this inside-outside relationship in *Sons and Lovers*. Lawrence writes about the father:

> He was shut out from all family affairs. No one told him anything. The children, alone with their mother told her all about the day's happenings, everything. Nothing had really taken place in them until it was told to their mother. But as soon as the father came in, everything stopped. He was like the scotch in the smooth, happy machinery of the home. And he was always aware of this fall of silence on his entry, the shutting off of life, the unwelcome. . . . He would dearly have liked the children to talk to him, but they could not.

When there was an attempt at closeness, this kind of father could not make contact. Nor could his son. Their alienation from each other had already gone too far. Again to quote D. H. Lawrence:

41

Paul won a prize in a competition in a child's paper. Everybody was highly jubilant.

"Now you'd better tell your father when he comes in," said Mrs. Morel. "You know how he carries on and says he's never told anything."

"All right," said Paul. But he would almost rather have forfeited the prize than have to tell his father.

"I've won a prize in a competition, dad," he said.

Morel turned round to him.

"Have you, my boy? What sort of a competition?"

"Oh, nothing—about famous women."

"And how much is the prize, then, as you've got?"

"It's a book."

"Oh, indeed!"

"About birds."

"Hm—hm!"

And that was all. Conversation was impossible between the father and any other member of the family. He was an outsider.

Many men I see in my practice had fathers who were figuratively absent, an outsider at home, and a lot more had fathers who were literally absent. Tragically, these fathers had died at an extremely early age. Their deaths were due to alcohol, diabetes, tuberculosis or heart attacks. They also died in accidents or World Wars. Still other men came from divorced parents. They too had grown up in their mother's custody and had no fathers at home.

Regardless of the reason—dead, divorced, indifferent, outsider or simply working too many hours a day —most of my generation, I think, suffered from this absent-father syndrome.

Aside from absent or nonexistent fathers, I think many men also grew up with negative models for fathers. Maybe the best example would be a father who was hypercritical. He may have been absent or present, rural or urban, active or passive. It didn't really matter. Above all, he was chronically dissatisfied with his son's efforts. Insecure and maybe even threatened by his son, this kind of father felt whatever the boy did, *it was never good enough.*

I hear men recall that as a child they came home from school with all B's and one C. Their father's reaction was always, "Why the C?" With all A's and a B+, his first question was sure to be, "What happened?" Or it was that mildly critical, "Oh, indeed" or "Hm—hm!"

I see many men in my office who recall building a model airplane at school or with their dads. And they can only remember their father's invariably saying, "The glue's on sloppy" or "The nails aren't reset right."

*It was never right.*

I see men who get their B.A.s and M.A.s and M.D.s and Ph.D.s. It's never enough. They make $20,000 or $50,000 or $150,000 a year. But it doesn't really matter if a man is still trying to get the approval he never received from a hypercritical father *or* mother, whose carping voice is still heard in his head.

I think a man's all-consuming effort to please his father has two obvious implications:

1. Growing up with an overly critical parent, a child suffers from low self-confidence and low self-esteem. He grows up to be as insecure as his father was.

2. Sons of hypercritical fathers also tend to put 100 percent of their energy into external "success." Little is left over for wife and family. Although these men may seem chauvinistic, I think it is simply that as they grew up, women were never given a high priority in their lives. Interpersonal relationships weren't important. Achievement and overachievement were everything. So twenty years later, it is not surprising these men enter marriage with absolutely no idea whatsoever of how to succeed in that marriage.

Although I have spoken in shorthand, the problem

of having a nonexistent or negative model is very real for most men. After all, we do learn our future roles from present models. And, if there is no model (or a negative model) how do boys learn to be men, husbands and fathers?

In psychotherapy I always ask the men I see: Who were the adult men in your life? If father was absent, literally or figuratively, was there an uncle or neighbor? An elder brother? A grandparent or a teacher? A coach or college professor? A clergyman? Do you see any heroes ten years older than you at work? Who, if anyone, provides a positive model?

More and more I hear men say they had and have no heroes. The majority, in fact, find it an idea that had never entered into their thoughts.

My concluding point about fathers is an obvious one. No one can do anything very well without going through a prior apprenticeship. I think it's very hard for a boy to become an active husband without having enjoyed such an apprenticeship. Yet the majority of husbands I see in my practice tell me they missed out on this opportunity.

•

*The libido of the American man is focused almost entirely upon his business so that as a husband he is glad to have no responsibilities. He gives the complete direction of his family life over to his wife. This is what you call giving independence to the American woman. It is what I call the laziness of the American man.*

Carl Jung
1912

One corollary of a nonexistent or negative father was a present mother. Indeed most of us were raised by our mothers. Our primary adult model was our mom. And she was often a strong, memorable woman.

Three kinds of mothers are frequently described by the men I see in my office who are their children: 1) Accepting women, 2) angry or rejecting women, and 3) disappointed women. Again, I am speaking in broad brush terms and drawing a composite picture.

The first kind of mother was a woman who accepted her husband and his way of life. Let's take for example a San Francisco, blue collar, Italian Catholic family with six children. The father worked hard all day and came home exhausted every night. Of course, the mother was perhaps even more exhausted. But it was perfectly all right with her for her husband to come home, take off his shoes, put up his feet, read the paper, have a couple of beers, eat silently through dinner, listen to the radio or watch television and fall asleep in his chair. (Meanwhile she fixed dinner, bathed children, washed dishes, read bedtime stories, prepared the next day's lunches for the children and scrubbed the kitchen floor.) After all, wasn't that how all couples lived?

These mothers respected their breadwinner husbands. And they taught their children that, basically, that was the way life was meant to be. If there was any anger underneath the surface, it was all well hidden. Mother's fundamental message was "Peace at any price."

In one sense, children of accepting mothers had fathers who were passive at home. And yet, dad's domestic image as king in his own castle was reinforced by mother. As these boys became men, they simply followed in their fathers' footsteps. Why not? What more did a wife want?

For such a man his own marriage proves to be a tremendous shock. Unlike mom, his wife doesn't see a man's (or a woman's) role that way at all. Not surprisingly, the wife demands her husband change his ways. But how does a man suddenly change after fifteen or twenty years of growing up with a passive father and an accepting mother?

The second kind of mother was not accepting, but rejecting. She was rejecting of both the husband and marriage. She stayed in the marriage "for the sake of the children." Or she didn't get divorced for economic or religious reasons. However, she was resentful of her predicament. In fact, she was furious, and she conveyed this fury to her children. Her message wasn't peace at any price. On the contrary, her bitterness and hostility toward her husband, the father, were direct. She waged open warfare.

Her message, overt and covert, was that "Men only want one thing." "They're all bastards." Or she said to her son, "You'll end up just like your father." She warned her daughter, "Whatever you do, don't marry a man like your father."

She constantly degraded the father (who stood for all men) in front of her children. She henpecked, nitpicked, overrode and overruled him in a million ways.

Let me ask: How can a son (or daughter) grow up on this battleground and not be injured? The boy with such a negative view of his father and, by extension, himself? The girl with a cynical view of her father, in particular, and men in general? Surely the problem of a passive, ineffectual man is compounded by an angry, undermining woman, and such a combination has to bode poorly for a child's future relationships with the opposite sex.

Many women I see come from this kind of family. They are most likely to have gone on to marry weak men. Later, they report hearing and hating their mother's voice inside themselves as they degrade their own husbands over and over and over.

The third kind of mother had a more complicated relationship with her husband and sons. She is more difficult to categorize, but she was described by psychologist Kenneth Keniston, in his first book, *The Uncommitted*.

The book described a group of Harvard students of a decade ago who were extremely bright and who all dropped out of school before graduation. Their failure to graduate from Harvard was, however, not for academic reasons. Their dropping out was due, instead, to a complex problem which existed between the boys' mothers and fathers. Later the problem was transferred from mother to son.

What was the problem?

To begin with: All of the boys' fathers had been idealists in their youth. They had usually come from an Ivy League college or an equally prestigious school. They had dreamed of going to Paris, becoming artists, or writing the great American novel. In fact, the mothers had married the fathers, at least in part, for their idealism.

But despite his family's high expectations for his future success, dad had not taken the path toward Paris or any other idealistic goal. He hadn't gone on to paint or write. He had instead taken a job directly on Wall Street and had become a successful stockbroker or lawyer. True, he had made money. But five or fifteen years into the marriage he, too, had become an absent father. And he had become a terrible disappointment to the mother.

The disappointed mother—and this was the crucial point—then transferred her expectations from the husband to the son. Not only did she transfer her expectations, but also her sexual energy—once directed toward the husband and marriage—was now poured into her son. It was a case of Oedipus-in-reverse. Her boy became the primary focus of her adoration and expectations. He became the symbol of her hopes and dreams. His life became the projection on which she placed not only the child's future, but her own future as well. Her life depended upon his achievements.

Mom's indirect pressure on her son (to be the idealist his father was not, to be the man his father was not) became just too great. As the boy approached success, the psychological stresses became overwhelming. So he dropped out. It was not a conscious decision. But rather than live out his mother's expectations for him, impossible expectations as he saw it, he became uncommitted. He also became detached, distant, withdrawn and cool. He became, in a word, passive.

This relationship among mother and father and son is not a new one. Nor is it limited to the university-trained or to the middle or upper classes. It cuts across all lines and economic levels. Again, we need only to look at the poor coal-mining family in D. H. Lawrence's *Sons and Lovers* to read a classic example. In this great novel, written over 65 years ago, Lawrence wrote about his own thinly disguised background:

The boy was small and frail at first, but he came on quickly. He was a beautiful child, with dark gold ringlets, and dark-blue eyes which changed gradually to a clear grey. His mother loved him passionately. He came just when her own bitterness of disillusion was hardest to bear; when her faith in life was shaken, and her soul felt dreary and lonely. She made much of the child, and the father was jealous. At last Mrs. Morel despised her husband. She turned to the child; she turned from the father . . .

The mother's turning from the husband to the son is a common story among the men I see today. It is also common that such a mother, like the others I've described, has helped to shape her son's future relationships. So here let me summarize the effect of these three kinds of mothers on their sons' future with other women.

The accepting kind of mother supported her passive husband, and their son grew up passive in his father's image. The angry, rejecting kind of mother undermined her husband, and since the son saw himself as an extension of his father, his view of himself as a man was likewise undermined. The disappointed kind of mother, who both directly and indirectly rejected their husband, eventually transferred her hopes and expectations from the husband to the son. These became impossible expectations for the boy so, rather than try to live up to them, he became detached and uncommitted.

There were large differences in these three kinds of mothers. Yet they tended to produce a common result. Most of their sons, insecure as boys in their own masculinity, turned into passive husbands.

•

*Those who do not remember the past are condemned to relive it.*

George Santayana

Today many boys are reliving history and continuing to grow up with absent fathers. Certainly the reasons are different from those in past eras, but the fact remains that the contemporary wife and mother often has little choice about an absent or ineffectual husband. Consequently, she often has no alternative but to fill the paternal vacuum created by our increasing numbers of absent fathers. Those numbers are growing and the statistics are sobering.

For example: One out of six children under eighteen in the United States lives with a single parent, usually his mother. This is almost double the number of twenty-five years ago. In addition, the number of annual divorces in the United States is more than twice the number of ten years ago, and over 60 percent of all divorces involve at least one child.

Passive husbands may be one cause for our divorce rate, but the increase in absent fathers is also one obvious result of those divorces. So, again, not only is there a male vacuum in a lot of today's homes, but a woman must play the extremely difficult role of being both mother and father to her children.

Here, my point is not that women are frequently and sadly left with that almost impossible job of being all things to all people. Rather, it is that single mothers do exist in large numbers today, and their children often grow up lacking ongoing and involved male models. In short, we are reliving history, and a new generation of boys, insecure in their own masculinity, continues to be produced at an increasingly rapid rate.

In terms of the current generation, I see high school and college students in my office who are very similar to those Harvard dropouts of a decade ago. These young men also look around and see no heroes, no male models they want to emulate in their own adult life.

As a case in point, I was recently invited to speak with a group of parents and students at a small private high school in northern California. (A school, I'm told, where 50 percent of the students come from divorced families.) For about an hour I spoke about absent fathers and present mothers.

The high school students in the audience immediately recognized and acknowledged the picture I had painted. Indeed, they quickly zeroed in on the pain of their own personal situation. One boy said with a simple eloquence:

"You've described my family perfectly. My father was the epitome of the passive man. For over ten years I watched him and my mother drive each other crazy. He kept getting further and further away until one day he finally left my mom for another woman, who happens to be about twenty years younger than my mother.

"After my father left home my mother changed a lot. She lost about twenty pounds and got very depressed. But then she came out of it, went back to school and is now O.K. She's still trying out new things and doesn't have much time for either my sister or me, but I can understand where she's coming from. Still, it's not been easy for any of us."

A seventeen-year-old boy added his support, but was angrier about his predicament. He said:

"My father also divorced my mother and left home a few years ago. Actually, I'm mad as hell at him for leaving. But he was passive, too, and all my mother's energies went (and are still going) into me.

"Now, I'm so angry at my father that I don't really like to be around him anymore. It's very strained between us and I also feel weird around other fathers. I just don't know how to act. I'm having a lot of trouble relating to the male teachers at school. I even went to a psychiatrist for help, but he was like a marshmallow. So I never went back after the second visit."

The boy's fifteen-year-old brother was sitting next to him and added:

"I feel the same way. Only, unlike my brother, I don't get good grades and try to please everyone. When I'm with my father I'm nice, but it's sort of an act. I'm much more comfortable with my mother. We're really close, but sometimes it's just too much and I can't wait to leave home."

A third boy with divorced parents summed up his situation:

"I'm also much closer to my mother and can tell her almost everything. And yet, although my father was passive, I still miss him and wish he were home. I'd like things to be different around the house, but they're not."

Clearly, these boys knew something was wrong at

51

home. In spite of current and popular misreadings to the contrary, these adolescents were saying they wanted and needed something they weren't getting from their mother and father. At some intuitive level, they knew there was something uniquely different to be gained from each of their parents.

Or as Eric Berne (author of *Games People Play*) once said:

There are frogs and there are princes and princesses. Mothers give sons permission to be a prince but the father must show him how. . . . Fathers give daughters permission to be princesses. And mothers must show them how. Otherwise, both boys and girls will grow up and always see themselves as frogs.

Maybe this generation of young men, like those Harvard dropouts of a decade ago, will see themselves as frogs. Without fathers to show them how to be princes, they will also become withdrawn, cool, detached and passive in their own adult lives.

On the other hand, there is another possibility. It is a possibility that is also rooted in a man's lack of a positive male model at home. It is an alternative pathway that a man can take today, but one which also begins with a male's insecurities about his own masculinity.

As I mentioned earlier, a man who is passive at home is often extremely active at work. On the job he is energetic and assertive. Indeed he may be absolutely dynamic. And yet as the old saying about the salesman goes, "He may be a tiger in the territory, but he's a mouse in the house."

Obviously there's a certain reality to a man's being a tiger at work. To get ahead in most jobs a man is expected to work the better part of every day. The size of his promotion or paycheck depends upon his production. A man's economic rewards relate to time spent at the office, not at home with his family. Consequently, should there be any free time, a man often takes a second job. He simply can't increase his paycheck by coming home early.

However, there's a less obvious reason for a man being driven during the day. And maybe it is time we moved from the mouse to tiger part, the assertive side of today's passive man. This side, too, can result from an absence of fathering. The lack of a positive male model at home can also produce an active man outside of an intimate relationship, but an active man who is still quite insecure about his own masculinity. He may look like a prince. But underneath the façade, he often feels like a frog.

This is a man who has an underlying need for acceptance and approval. He is a man who may be overly assertive as one means of defending against his own underlying insecurities.

It is extremely important that we understand this relationship between excessively aggressive men and their insecurities. It is important, because when we speak about the tiger and mouse parts of a man, I think we are frequently talking about two sides of the same coin.

Today, and in the extreme, we do see a kind of man who is superactive because of his low self-esteem and unstable self-confidence. He feels that if he is not a great hero, he is nothing. His quest for approval and acceptance is a full-time job. His achievements are all-consuming.

Actually, we have a superb case history of just such a man. He is a thirty-three-year-old male who displays a wide variety of the symptoms I've just described. However, he is not my patient. Rather, his psychiatrist is a mythical man named Doctor Spielvogel. This fictional patient is, of course, Alexander Portnoy of Philip Roth's modern American classic *Portnoy's Complaint*.

Although the hero is Jewish, his story could just as easily be the lament of any Catholic or Protestant, Greek or Armenian, Polish or Italian frog trapped in the body of a thirty-three-year-old would-be prince. In his free associations and continuous complaint, Alexander Portnoy tells Doctor Spielvogel (and us) in great detail exactly how it feels to be so insecure.

Regarding his absent, ineffectual father Alex Portnoy says that in addition to other things he is just beginning to suspect about his father, "He isn't King Kong."

About his mother, Alex says (among other things) that it was she who could accomplish anything. "What radar on that woman! And this is *before* radar!"

On his need for a positive male model, he tells his psychiatrist that he can't stand being frightened over nothing. He begs his doctor to bless him with manhood. "Make me brave! Make me strong! Make me *whole!*"

On his being a tiger in public life, he reviews his accomplishments as the Assistant Commissioner of Human Opportunity for the City of New York. And he adds: "I graduated first in my law school class! Remember? I have graduated first from every class I've ever *been* in! . . . I am a highly respected man in my profession, that should be obvious!"

But within this would-be prince lie serious doubts. He knows that professionally he is going somewhere, but privately, what has he got to show for himself?

What Alex Portnoy has to show, of course, are insecurities and defenses against those insecurities, public successes and private failures and—because of his underlying insecurities about manhood—a need to prove himself which is certainly compounded with women.

His attempts to be a sexual tiger are not unfamiliar to us. Like so many would-be Don Juans, Alex must compulsively seduce a different woman every time he gets a chance. He does so not only to confirm his own masculinity. He must also seduce many women because he is afraid of getting too close to any one woman. As he laments:

> You see, I just can't stop! Or tie myself to any *one*. I have affairs that last as long as a year, a year and a half, months and months of love, both tender and voluptuous, but in the end—it is as inevitable as death—time marches on and lust peters out. In the end, I just cannot take that step into marriage.

Accordingly, in a marriage or outside it, a seeming tiger like Alexander Portnoy is often continually preoccupied with women. In fact, he may be obsessed with them and continually dominate them in acts of incessant, but relatively meaningless, intercourse.

And why? Because underneath he is just too preoccupied with himself. Alexander Portnoy is the center of his own universe. His own narcissism is rampant. As Alex says: "Vanity? Why not! . . . That's what's so nice about growing up! You want to take? You take!"

And take he does! With an endless series of women he takes and takes. But it is never enough. On the subject of love, he sums it all up: "Love? Spelled l-u-s-t! Spelled s-e-l-f! . . . You whiner." And ultimately, "Oh, so alone! Nothing but *self!* Locked in *me!*"

Most women have met this kind of man whose main preoccupation is with "me, myself and I." He is the sort of fellow who primps and preens not only in front of the mirrors of the world, but in front of the world itself. His narcissism is worse than any woman's. He is a man today who struts around like a bantam rooster or, perhaps more accurately, like a peacock spreading and admiring his own feathers. He is a man who must prove himself and incessantly admire his own image at every chance.

The trouble is that today's proliferation of peacocks (as well as passive men) is multiplying and getting worse. Why? Because today's men are in a state of confusion and are increasingly insecure about their own masculinity. The man's role is unclear. His models are scarce. His identity is tenuous.

At work, once a traditional source for a strong masculine identity, he finds that meaningful jobs are extremely rare and even disappearing. At home, he doesn't know whether he is coming or going. His wife always seems to be cutting him down to size. (Whereas the real problem is that he already feels too small in his own house.)

It adds up to more and more men's confidence being at an all-time low. And unfortunately, for men and women alike, the man's resulting low self-confidence forces him to become even more extreme in the two types of behavior I have just described.

Insecure, he becomes either more passive in the face of current confusion over a proper male role or, defending himself against that confusion and his own insecurities, he becomes more selfish and self-centered. He becomes as narcissistic as Alexander Portnoy. And he tries desperately to prove his manhood with many women because he is afraid of getting too close to one woman.

Neither kind of man—narcissistic or passive (or both)—is particularly appealing to most women. Nor do these traits do anything to reduce the current friction that exists today between men and women. On the contrary, both extremely passive and excessively macho men serve to increase that friction. They only cause women to go wilder and that, of course, leads to a worsening of the underlying problem. In the face of a woman's wildness the insecure male—active or passive—only becomes more insecure, more defensive.

If we are not to repeat history, must we not learn from it? For example, am I right in assuming that a good man is hard to find today? And, if so, why? How important are fathers in America? How necessary are

56

they, not only for sons, but daughters? What are we doing to prepare and encourage fathers to spend more time at home? Could we do more economically and educationally? Must we not recognize the need for positive male models under whom a child can experience an adequate apprenticeship? Must we not also interrupt the continuing battle between the sexes? And, as a first step, can we not begin by changing the current climate which exists between men and women?

Is not that climate filled today with mutual mistrust, anger and even paranoia? Does not that paranoia, in turn, bring out the worst in us? Does it not increase both a man *and* woman feeling pressured? Do we not then respond to each other's defenses?

The man responds to a woman's anger. She responds to his passivity. He responds to her unhappiness. She responds to his narcissism. He reacts to her bitchiness. She reacts to his machismo. Each person responds to the other's defense against his or her own underlying fears and insecurities. In short, we keep bringing out and reacting to each other's worst side. Once again, we have met the enemy and he is us!

# PART III

# In Defense of Women

•

*The opposite of love is not hate, it's apathy.*

Rollo May
*Love and Will*

Let us again return to the original problem. I said a wild wife married to a passive man is fed up with the evening routine. She complains that her husband comes home late and tired, reads his paper, eats silently through dinner, watches too much television, never talks and pays only token attention to her.

Not infrequently, she's also angry that he doesn't do his share at home. He won't fix broken toilets, carry out garbage and pick up his dirty socks. A whole laundry list of minor complaints. (I hasten to add that with many women, "I wish you'd not leave your dirty socks on the floor" means only "I wish you'd not leave your dirty socks on the floor." With other women, however, "He never helps me" means "He's never home to help me.") To put it simply, I think the common complaints familiar to most of us are often the tip of an enormous iceberg.

Early in Sheila Ballantyne's novel *Norma Jean the*

*Termite Queen,* the heroine describes the feelings of many seemingly wild women today. She says:

> I sometimes stop suddenly and realize I'm scream-
> ing all the time, or angry in a way I've never been
> angry before. It's an insidious thing, creeps over you
> and has you in its throes before you even realize
> what brought it on. I am speaking of a rage so in-
> articulate that to even attempt to describe it is to
> court accusations of insanity.

The questions are: What is the meaning of this in-articulate rage? What lies beyond such a woman's apparent wildness?

Like Norma Jean, many a wife today may be extremely angry, but I am convinced that beneath the rage and tears, she is also depressed. That's the real iceberg.

Her depression may be marked by anxiety, or a vague feeling that something's wrong. It may express itself as boredom or an overall inability to cope. As Norma Jean describes it:

> I don't know what's wrong with me lately. I can't
> seem to make out the grocery list. I start it, the way
> I always do, but can't seem to keep up my interest.
> Lettuce. Peanut butter. Bread. Then it trails off. I
> find I've been staring into space a lot and can't seem
> to concentrate.

Depression may include symptoms of decreased concentration. It may also include diminished sexual appetite and increased physical ailments: back pain, migraines, constipation, heartburn, stomach trouble, or menstrual cramps. It can be expressed as restlessness, insomnia, weight gain or weight loss. It appears as lethargy, listlessness and a lack of energy. It involves the feeling, "I don't know what's the matter. But I'm tired all the time." Commonly it involves a problem with alcohol or an affair.

I think the reasons for a woman's depression in a relationship with a man are complex. But let me simplify and describe five major causes of depression which I hear repeatedly described by women in my office.

## Expectations

The first cause of depression has to do with expectations. Understandably, most women have high hopes for a relationship and yet the distance often turns out to be tremendous between expectations and reality. In fact, the higher a woman's expectations, the louder the crash when she is brought down to the realities of daily living.

Most of us know the feeling when reality does not live up to expectations. For example, we come out of a Saturday night movie and think, "I shouldn't have read all those rave reviews. Nothing could have been that good!" Or we come back from a disappointing vacation and say, "My hopes were too high. I should have been more realistic."

On a more charged and sexual level I hear a common refrain about the singles' bar scene. A person picks up a stranger and has a one-night stand. The next morning's reaction is usually, "The fantasy was better than the reality. Maybe I'll know better next time."

Suffice it to say, we easily recover from a mediocre movie or disappointing vacation. We even bounce back after an unrewarding one-night stand. Nothing is permanently lost. But a lot is lost when a wife (or husband) feels cornered in a less than rewarding marriage. Something vital is lost when there is chronic disappointment day after day after day.

Here is a rather extended illustration of how the expectations a woman brings to marriage can lead to disappointment, frustration, wildness and an eventual depression. These expectations are a kind of psychological baggage that a lot of women still carry with them, consciously or unconsciously, into their adult lives.

The basic expectation begins with a girl's growing up hearing her mother's (or father's or society's) message, "Marry well." The implication is: "And then you'll be happy."

The problem is, of course, that after marrying "well" the woman isn't always happy. On the contrary, her life is not often the bowl of cherries that it's been advertised to be. In fact such high expectations, like those rave reviews, only serve to make more disappointing the actual realities of her eventual marriage.

More specifically, I have known many women who did well in school, played sports, were popular, developed a variety of talents and held excellent jobs. But, at least on one level, it was all a kind of bait. The woman's achievements were really secondary to the hidden agenda and primary goal of catching a good man. Directly or indirectly these women were following their mother's admonition and putting a tremendous amount of energy into finding Mr. Right.

As a case in point, I know a nurse who left Muncie, Indiana, because most of her high school friends and nursing school classmates were marrying local boys. They were settling down to a predictable life in a small midwestern town that the nurse had enjoyed as a child, but which she was trying to escape as an adult.

Upon leaving home, the nurse's mother said in effect,

"Look, you'll probably marry in the next few years. So pick a location to live where you can meet some decent and available men." Just for good measure the mother added, "And don't end up in Washington or San Francisco. In those two cities the ratio of single women to eligible men is ten to one!"

With such ratios ringing in her ears the nurse spent the next six years holding hospital jobs in Chicago, Seattle and Honolulu. She kept going west because she was supposedly bored at work. But in fact, she was seeking new frontiers because she simply wasn't meeting any worthwhile men.

Like a fairy tale, however, the story did seem to have a happy ending. In Honolulu the nurse met and married her current husband, who was then a second-year medical student. Ironically, this happy ending was only the beginning of yet another, and rather unfortunate, story. What happened?

Initially the nurse poured a tremendous amount of energy into her husband and marriage. She genuinely believed that her man was her window on life. Indeed, her life was essentially a series of reactions to his actions. Her needs were secondary to his goals. Consequently, in those early years, she continued to work full time and support her husband through medical school.

And not only four years of medical school. The woman also went on to provide the major economic support during her husband's year of internship and six years of a surgical residency (during which time she had three children). In addition, she functioned as a significant force behind her husband's eventual rise in the world of medicine. In short, the message and expectation to marry well had paid off for the nurse.

Or had it?

Looking back, it was clear that in the early years of marriage she and her husband had shared a common struggle. They had worked together. Her husband came home exhausted, but as a student and young doctor he still had time to talk and his wife always made time to listen. The reality was that she offered wise counsel and he usually took her advice. Yet with the physician's ultimate success, life changed dramatically for both husband and wife.

After ten years of marriage and three children the husband stopped coming home and asking for his wife's opinion. He didn't need her help. In fact, when she complained about their deteriorating marriage, he went so far as to tell her, "Don't bother me with all the communication bullshit. Just remember, my time is now worth over $100 an hour!"

Meanwhile, if the wife did express her unhappiness and frustration, her husband would repeatedly reply, "The trouble is (my dear) you've lost your femininity." (It was, of course, the lowest blow.)

Then, too, there was an everpresent threat. If his wife didn't shape up he would leave her. He would find a woman who would appreciate and understand him. A woman who would appreciate the material rewards of being a doctor's wife. A more "feminine" woman who wouldn't always be on his back.

Needless to say, the wife in this marriage felt wild for obvious reasons. She also felt cheated by the expectations with which she had entered marriage: Marry well. Live through your husband and you'll be happy. Let your man be your window on life.

She had certainly followed her mother's admonitions. She had lived by the rules and played the game. She had lived through her husband. And what had happened? He was now too busy to give her the time of day!

The nurse, who was now in her early forties, felt not only angry and cheated, trapped and depressed— but also she felt *used*. The reality was that fifteen years into this particular marriage, the nurse was also almost totally dependent on her husband for economic support. She had progressively given up her own career to raise their three children and had not kept up with her nursing. Consequently, when she did consider a divorce, she knew it would not be easy to go back to school, take refresher courses, look for part-time work, and still continue to do the kind of job she expected of herself in raising her children. The economic and psychological price of a divorce would be extremely costly.

In addition, her husband was just reaching his prime as an attractive man, but what happened to her prime as an attractive woman?

Put mildly, it was not the life she had expected. Nor was it one that she would have chosen for herself. And it was certainly not a position this nurse, wife and mother wanted to be in after fifteen years of marriage. Was it any wonder she was so devastated and depressed?

## Energy

I think there is a second reason for a woman's depression. It is also best illustrated by a case history.

An intelligent and successful journalist that I know entered marriage with a clear view of her role as a wife. It was a view similar to the nurse's in the previous story. The journalist also had an old-fashioned view of marriage. She was totally committed to pleasing her husband. No fifty-fifty contracts. No *quid pro quo*. No rigid rules such as she does the dishes and he carries out the garbage. Or she cooks on Tuesday, Thursday and Saturday; he cooks on Monday, Wednesday and Friday. On the contrary, even after eight to ten hours on another job, she looked forward to the role of being a traditional wife.

For two years she cheerfully came home, kept house and cooked gourmet meals. There were no power struggles over who picked up dirty laundry or socks. (There were no struggles simply because she did it all.) And yet the wife did have her needs. She wanted to be able to talk with her husband.

However, when she did try to discuss her day's writing project or tomorrow's interview, her husband would routinely turn on the news if it happened to be 7 o'clock. Or in her mid-sentence, he'd pick up the evening paper. When she asked about his own day, he begged off because of Monday night football. When she wanted to make love, he wanted to stay up for a late movie.

After five years the journalist concluded, "My husband and I have different passion levels in the marriage." And it was true. But what could she do?

The second cause for a woman's depression relates to this last comment about the writer's and her husband's "passion levels'" being different. Passion levels are higher for most women than men in marriage, but again there's a kicker. A woman's depression is increased when she realizes that her husband does indeed have passion and energy. It is simply that he does not have energy for her.

The husband I have described arrives home at night with his reservoirs empty; he's expended everything he has. He's spent all his available resources on other people and external causes. He's drained absolutely dry. Or is he?

On weekends that same husband does have the energy to play tennis, go hunting, fishing, bowling, golfing, jogging, boating or skiing—but usually not with his wife, even if she had the urge to participate. So it is not so surprising that his wife feels not only cheated, but depressed. It is not enough that her husband provokes her by giving so little of himself at home. He compounds the problem by flaunting the energy he expends elsewhere.

Day after day, the wife sees her husband pouring all of his excess energy into what for him is a whole series of less frightening, more unambivalently rewarding causes than their marriage.

For example, the wildest women I know are likely to have husbands who can be extremely warm with other people: friends, colleagues, acquaintances, other family members, even total strangers. The wife watches the generosity with which her husband gives of himself to these other people, and it's precisely because there is so little left over for her that she ultimately feels hurt, rejected and furious. If the wife were not to witness her husband's capacity for generosity and warmth, maybe she could make do with the minimal quota he has for her. But the contrast is too much, and understandably, she gets depressed.

## Control

The third reason for depression has to do with a phrase I've used throughout the book. It relates to a woman's wanting "something more" from a man. I think we are now in a better position to understand this request, so let us return to the wife's complaints that a man doesn't carry his share of the domestic load. He doesn't wash dishes, help with children, do diapers, vacuum rugs, pick up his dirty socks—that laundry list. Arguments over dirty socks or dirty dishes can lead to tremendous power struggles. They can unleash torrents of unmitigated rage. They can become a ticket of admission into therapy or into a divorce.

However, I do hear more and more about the husband who does try to please his wife in these matters. He doesn't forget to carry out the garbage. He fixes broken toilets. He does dishes, vacuums rugs and even picks up his dirty socks. In fact, he twists and turns himself into a pretzel trying to accommodate this week's request from his wife. He becomes a chameleon at home. She turns red, he turns red. She is blue, he's blue.

The paradox is, although he may do dishes three nights a week or vacuum rugs on weekends, his wife still may not be placated. In fact, the man being a good soldier, carrying out orders, following the laundry list, may only serve to compound the problem by having his wife's demands increase.

Personally, I think when such a wife keeps goading her husband it's because, unconsciously, she is actually threatened by the control she is developing over him. The control and power to get him to behave as she wants. The husband's repeatedly giving in to her is further evidence that he is indeed a passive and easily manipulated man. That he is a "wet noodle," a chameleon.

In a sense the wife provokes her husband, and she may constantly provoke him, to test his limits and to test his ability to remain himself.

It is true that provoking a husband often leads to arguments. (Over those dirty dishes or socks or whatever.) These are often violent arguments. But the fact is that although sometimes destructive, they can also serve a constructive purpose in this kind of marriage.

The inevitable fight not only releases tension, but also forces the husband to state what he thinks and how he feels. It involves him with his wife at a feeling level. Like good sex, a good argument means that a husband is finally active, involved and engaged with his wife. It is tangible proof that he can be strong. In the midst of a battle, he is no longer a wet noodle.

Between battles, however, what happens to the ongoing power struggles in such a marriage? More specifically, what happens to the woman who wants her husband to take more responsibility and assume more leadership at home?

In my office I've heard of some rather surprising results. Indeed, once the issue of control is defined and this aspect of a wife's anger is understood, it does not always ensure smooth sailing. On the contrary, there may still be resistance when a husband initially acts in a more decisive way. For example, here are two brief illustrations of what often happens.

A wife complains that her husband doesn't spend enough time with their son on weekends. So he announces he's going to take the boy to the beach on Saturday afternoon. What's her response? "The ocean in November?" (You idiot.) Of course his reaction may be to say "forget it" and not take the boy at all.

The second example: A wife complains her husband watches the late news on TV in bed instead of making love to her. So one night he unexpectedly turns off the set, rolls over, and begins to nibble at her ear. Her first reaction? It could well be, "Are you kidding?" or "What are you doing?" or "Don't, darling, I'm exhausted." But again she *may* just be testing him. Does he really desire her, or is he just going through the motions? Unhappily, the chances are he'll just react passively (and furiously), mutter a favorite four- or fourteen-letter word to himself, roll over and fall asleep.

His being discouraged, in turn, simply confirms his wife's worst fear. Her husband is a wet noodle. He is too easily discouraged. And what is worse—he's apathetic.

The wife fears apathy. She fears that her husband really isn't that interested or he would stand up for what he wants and assert himself in positive ways. He wouldn't always let her dominate. He would fight for his ideas and for her. If he really loved his woman, he wouldn't be so damned passive.

My point is that a wife will still fight. As much as she wants her husband to be more active, there is something in her that will automatically resist giving up control. She will initially try to undermine his efforts. But, in a very real sense, her reaction is a test, and if he is to pass that test—he must stick to his decision. He must prove that he has values and is capable of standing up for those values and himself. He must show that he is emotionally strong and actively involved. He must demonstrate that he's capable of asserting himself. He must prove he's not apathetic.

Edward Albee has a perfect ear for the power struggles over control between a husband and wife. Therefore, it is not surprising what a "wild" Martha tells a "passive" George about her underlying depression in *Who's Afraid of Virginia Woolf?*

*Martha:*   You know what's happened, George? You want to know what's really happened? (Snaps her fingers) It's snapped finally. Not me . . . it. The whole arrangement. You can go along . . . forever, and everything's . . . manageable. You make all sorts of excuses to yourself . . . you know . . . this is life . . . the hell with it . . . maybe tomorrow he'll be dead . . . maybe tomorrow you'll be dead . . . all sorts of excuses. But then, one day, one night, something happens . . . and SNAP! It breaks. And you just don't give a damn anymore. I've tried with you, baby . . . really, I've tried.

*George:*   Come off it, Martha.

*Martha:*   I've tried . . . I've really tried.

*George:* (With some awe) You're a monster . . . you are.

*Martha:* I'm loud, and I'm vulgar, and I wear the pants in this house because somebody's got to, but I am not a monster. I am not.

# Isolation

The next reason for a woman's depression has to do with her sense of isolation. The isolation may stem from her husband's apathy and passivity at home. It may follow from her own initially high expectations and ensuing disappointments. It may result from her husband's putting all of his energies elsewhere. Whatever the reason, there's little doubt that a woman's isolation is certainly compounded by her ultimately feeling depressed in her own home.

Who could be lonelier and more isolated than a woman (or a man) living under the same roof (and in the same bed) with a partner to whom she (or he) is no longer speaking in a meaningful way?

And yet what I mean by a woman's isolation actually goes back further than the immediate relationship with her husband. It pertains more specifically, although not exclusively, to wives who are full-time homemakers. And it goes back to a woman's traditional support systems.

To review briefly, in previous eras a woman could rely upon a predictable group of people and institutions to offer affirmation and support for her way of life. For example, living in a rural area or stable neighborhood, a woman often had an extended family (grandmothers, sisters, cousins, and aunts) with whom to share her day. There was also the church and church community. There were old friends and familiar neighbors. Thus, most women of past generations had a rather extensive support system which offered them a sense of community and closeness. The system provided a woman with a large measure of the individual approval that she, like most of us, needed in her daily life.

Today, however, life has changed. There has been a rapid breakdown of traditional support systems. Extended families and intact neighborhoods have disappeared in the majority of urban and suburban settings. Life's pace has quickened. People are on the move. Twenty percent of Americans change homes every year and 50 percent move every five years. People and families today have obviously become more mobile, fragmented and isolated.

What is the result?

The man may still have his work ("Be a good provider . . .") as a place to get some measure of approval and applause. But his urban or suburban wife at home who is uprooted every few years and is increasingly isolated misses out on that measure of approval.

She may describe her feelings of isolation as a nagging need to call someone. She may describe it as feeling adrift and detached from the world. Sometimes she experiences the isolation as a vague sense of unreality, an undercurrent that something is missing in her life.

Sadly, many things are missing. The fact is that the isolated wife today seldom has close family members, long-standing friends or institutional traditions and rituals available to her. Consequently, who is the person most available to diminish her sense of isolation? Who is the major source of her daily support and approval?

Is it really surprising that such a wife turns to her husband, especially when he comes home at night for that approval? And just as she turns to him, her husband turns away. He feels the pressures at work are already enough for him, and his wife's adding increasing pressures at home is seen as just too much. Not only can't he understand why his wife wants that "something more" but he simply can't provide it. He feels he is being overwhelmed.

Consequently, many a modern woman is left with a vacuum for what was once a vital and extended support system in her life. She does not receive much help from her husband. In fact, at home she tends to be ignored rather than applauded. She is undermined rather than appreciated. With the result that the wife becomes immobilized. Her self-confidence is lowered rather than raised and her feelings of isolation and depression are further compounded.

How is a full-time homemaker and mother of small children likely to cope if she is excessively isolated at home all day?

Many women in this position find it extremely helpful to share their feelings with other women. These other women are usually young mothers who also spend most of their days wiping noses, drying tears, cleaning diapers and picking up toys.

For example, a lot of women with small children tell me that the highlight of their day is often a trip to the park. It is their therapy. The park bench is their therapist. Misery loves company and on a park bench a young mother can not only commiserate, but learn she isn't alone. She can also diminish her sense of isolation and get some much-needed support from other women for her vital role of mothering.

Some working women report a similar sense of personal isolation. For instance, a female doctor friend recently told me that she felt women's groups often serve a dual purpose. Professional associations, therapy sessions, night classes, weekend seminars, neighborhood clubs, hiking groups—the names really don't matter. What does matter is that a woman can not only discuss professional issues with her own peers in such groups, but after the tumult and shouting dies, she can also discuss personal problems.

As the doctor said, "My own group usually ends up on the same note. Our frustrations." She added, "Actually I think the real function of our getting together is not only to discuss official issues of common concern. It's also to share a communal depression."

Another observation concerning isolation and a communal depression comes from that patient of mine who works as an advertising executive. She was the person who observed that most of her women friends can make an easier transition than their husbands from work life to home life so that they, too, want "something more" at night. Recently she told me about her own sense of isolation at home. She thought that her isolation was common to women who were involved in full-time jobs and careers outside the house. Here's what she said:

"I find that most of my women friends who work have the same experience as I. They work as hard as their husbands, often harder, and yet when they come home, their husbands are much less communicative than they are. What happens? We women start a telephone syndicate. I call Pat, Pat calls Doris, Doris calls Sally, Sally calls me. If we cannot talk with our husbands, then we will share our daily experiences with each other."

There's more, I think, to this advertising executive's description of her telephone syndicate than meets the eye.

According to American Telephone and Telegraph, the telephone is primarily a woman's instrument. Historically, this has been true because women have spent more time than men in their homes during the day.

And yet, with more women working on jobs outside the home, one would expect the phone to be used less at night by women. However, that is not the case. Women are still not only the primary users of the telephone when they're at home, day or night, but also the phone continues to be used just as much, or more than in the past.

Personally, I think that "Pat calls Doris and Doris calls Sally" for a very significant reason today. Out-groups have always defended themselves by banding together and forming in-groups. In numbers there is strength. That's what support systems are all about. So that the out-group, in this case women, forms an in-group. They form a telephone syndicate, a bush telegraph, a communications network.

This network gives a woman a sense of communion as well as communication. It affords her an opportunity to share her life's experiences (because her husband can't or won't participate sufficiently in the sharing). Talking to other women she can get some support, sympathy and approval for everyday life experiences. She is not so isolated and alone.

In short, by reaching out to other women she is trying to get, albeit not from her husband, a bit of the "something more" she so desperately wants. She is reaching out for a sense of self-confidence and self-respect. A feeling of companionship and closeness. And in the process she is overcoming her isolation and dealing in a historically effective way with that communal depression.

# Ambivalence

The foregoing discussion about expectations, energy, passion, apathy and isolation leads to a final reason for a woman's depression. It relates to an obvious conclusion about married life. Today's wife is frequently left with contradictory feelings in her marriage. At home she must balance a whole variety of conflicting feelings about herself and her husband.

For example, a wife today has needs for independence and dependence, control and giving up control, communication and privacy. She has, in a word, extremely ambivalent feelings. Such feelings often lead to a state of confusion about the marriage itself. She wonders: To make compromises or insist on changes at home? To work on those changes or accept the status quo? To stay in the relationship or get out of it?

Such ambivalence and inner confusion, unfortunately, only serve to increase a woman's underlying sense of isolation and depression.

So it is not by accident that many groups to whom a woman turns for answers today speak primarily to one side of her ambivalence, and can easily be counterproductive to the other side. They speak in the strongest possible language to *either* her desire for independence *or* dependence, tough-mindedness *or* tenderness, marriage *or* going-it-alone.

To be more specific about currently popular answers for women. At one end of the spectrum, some women are attracted to Marabel Morgan's *Total Woman*. Mrs. Morgan clearly offers comfort in a wife's going back to the old and established expectation: "Live your life through your husband and you'll be happy." In her book, Mrs. Morgan speaks to the dependent-submissive side of a woman's ambivalence. For example, she writes:

It is only when a woman surrenders her life to her husband, reveres and worships him, and is willing to serve him, that she becomes really beautiful to him.

Mrs. Morgan goes on to assign four tasks to a wife who wants to be the total woman (the 4 A's):
1. Accept your husband just as he is.
2. Admire your husband every day.
3. Adapt to his way of life.
4. Appreciate all he does for you.

This simple advice, I think, hits at the very core of *one side* of a woman's ambivalence. That is, a wife's desire to nurture and be dependent upon a good man.

But what about the assertive-independent end of the spectrum? What about the wife who has adored her husband while he's put his energies elsewhere? What about the wife whose husband has been allergic to closeness, who hasn't been able or willing to love her in return? What about women who are just plain outraged at all men?

It is precisely such women who turn to another side of their ambivalent feelings. Dependence gives way to independence. Tenderness to tough-mindedness. Feeling like a slave to wanting to be a new kind of a master. The message is "To hell with the bastards, we'll live without them. I'm totally self-sufficient anyway."

For such a constellation of feelings, conscious or unconscious, there is another prescription. This advice comes from an earlier cutting edge of the women's movement. It also appeals in no uncertain terms to a single side of a woman's ambivalence. For example, Germaine Greer writes in *The Female Eunuch:*

One of the deepest evils in our society is tyrannical nurturance.

If independence is a necessary concomitant of freedom, women must not marry.

Compare these two appeals. They clearly reflect, I think, a woman's love-hate dependent-independent ambivalence toward men and marriage. (And let us also recall that both *The Total Woman* and *The Female Eunuch* became bestsellers in their time. Each struck a nerve, hit basic feelings, and offered clear answers to complex problems for a large readership.)

Here is a random sampling of prescriptions from Marabel Morgan and Germaine Greer.

### The Total Woman

Love and marriage is a commitment. Commitment involves a woman's full surrender to her man.

### The Female Eunuch

The cunt must come into its own.

### The Total Woman

If you want to free him to express his thoughts and emotions, begin by filling up his empty cup with admiration.

### The Female Eunuch

If women are to effect a significant amelioration in their condition it seems obvious that they must refuse to marry.

### The Total Woman

Perhaps you're like many women who say "I'm sorry, I can't be available. I have seven kids, four carpools, and I'm overworked." I have known bitter and frazzled housewives who have been transformed into calm and gentle Total Women!

### The Female Eunuch

The plight of mothers is more desperate than that of other women, and the more numerous the children the more hopeless the situation seems to be.

### The Total Woman

You have the power to lift your family spirit or bring it down to rock bottom. The atmosphere in your home is set by you.

### The Female Eunuch

Most women still need a room of their own and the only way to find it may be outside their own homes.

### The Total Woman

Adapting to his activities, his friends, and his food is not always easy, but it's right.

### The Female Eunuch

Many men are almost as afraid of abandonment, of failing as husbands as their wives are, and a woman who is not terrified of managing on her own can manipulate this situation.

## The Total Woman

Sincerely tell him "Thank You" with your attitudes, actions, and words. Give him your undivided attention, and try not to make any telephone calls after he comes home, especially after 8:00 P.M.

## The Female Eunuch

She must not allow herself to be ridiculed and baffled by arguments with her husband, or to be blackmailed by his innocence on his part in her plight.

## The Total Woman

Women need to be loved; men need to be admired. We women would do well to remember this one important difference between us and the other half.

## The Female Eunuch

The world will not change overnight and liberation will not happen unless individual women agree to be outcasts, eccentrics, perverts and whatever the powers-to-be choose to call them.

Is it really so surprising that these two groups of women can't understand each other? That they not only don't understand each other, but they engage in open warfare? They do so because to follow one set of strict guidelines and ignore the other, a woman must deny a major part of her own ambivalent personality.

For example, the woman who chooses to be totally dependent must ignore her needs for independence. She must negate the need for her own identity. Whereas at the other extreme, a woman who elects to be independent at all costs must repress her needs for tenderness and dependence. She must deny any need to be submissive (at least with a man). Because one group mirrors the other group's denied feelings, I think both sides feel not only threatened, they feel absolutely outraged at the other's prescription.

Why do these prescriptions continue to have such strong appeal to so many women today?

One reason is that we are in a time of great change and rapid transition. A woman's role is unclear. Her identity is confused and her new image not yet formed. Consequently, many a woman today is conflicted about what she "should" want and what she actually does want in her life. Put another way, there is often a vast difference between how a woman feels she *should be/would like to be/and is* at work and home. Her inner and outer worlds are seldom in harmony. Is it any wonder that answers which speak to one side of her ambivalence and ignore the other side are so appealing? At least they are clear!

And yet we must ask if either extreme really speaks to the true complexity and depth of feminine feelings. Does either prescription truly solve a woman's major dilemmas? For example, in a marriage some of those dilemmas are: How does a wife integrate her contradictory feelings in her daily life? How does she deal with the conflicting parts of her own personality during these times of transition? How does she express her conflicts and not always blame her husband for them? Furthermore, if she wants her man to make changes in a marriage, can she also make changes? Can she relax a little bit and begin seeing things from his point of view? Can she express anger at her husband and still find ways to admire him? Can she be assertive and still be feminine? In short, can she accept her ambivalence and play many roles in a good relationship?

The answers to these questions cannot be simple ones because the solutions for most women that I see don't lie in any single direction. For example, I do not believe the answer lies with a woman's suddenly becoming *either* a slave *or* the master. Either being a scapegoat *or* making her man the scapegoat.

I do believe that the answer begins with a woman's trying to recognize her own basic complexities and contradictory feelings. It begins with the woman allowing herself to wear many hats in a relationship. After all, it is not a question of *either/or*. A woman should be able to be *both* independent *and* dependent, active *and* passive, relaxed *and* serious, practical *and* romantic, tender *and* tough-minded, thinking *and* feeling, dominant *and* submissive.

So, obviously, should a man!

# PART IV

---

# The Problem Revisited

•

*When (Gertrude Stein) had come out of the anesthetic her mind was clear enough to formulate for the last time the simple yet inexhaustible problem to which she had addressed the energies of a lifetime of scientific curiosity and aesthetic adventure. "What is the answer?" she asked. There had never been a reply to satisfy her, and finally and again there was none. "In that case," she said, "what is the question?"*

J. M. Brinnin
*The Third Rose: Gertrude Stein and Her World*

The question is: Why are male and female differences under such heavy attack lately? Why does it seem so radical today to say that a lot of husbands and wives have different needs at night? That men and women are, in part, different animals?

Many of the reasons go back to my earlier comments. Man's fear of woman. The Industrial Revolution. A machine age which robbed men of their traditional roles and vital defenses. The increasing number of working wives. And ultimately, the current women's liberation movement.

At some intuitive level, men have always feared

that women could dominate and destroy them. As I said, this fear was universally expressed as distrust. The proverbs from all countries—Occidental and Oriental, ancient and modern—repeat this theme over and over. In 800 B.C. Homer wrote, "No trust is to be placed in women." Almost 3,000 years later a Black American song tells us, "Ashes to ashes, dust to dust, never seen a woman a man could trust." So too the Victorian saying "Keep the woman in her place" was undoubtedly an initial unconscious response to man's vague awareness that he was about to lose his physical advantage. Machines would in the future work equally well for both sexes.

Of course, man's fear and distrust also kept women in their place not only at home, but at work. However, by the 1960s, women's rage finally reached a boiling point. It did so, I think, for two basic reasons:

1. At home the wife no longer had eight children to consume her energies. So she wanted a more active husband and lively relationship. Instead she found herself living with a passive husband in a boring marriage, and it made her furious.

2. At work she found herself trying to compete in a man's world with an arm and leg tied behind her back. She found herself handicapped in hiring practices, promotion policies and pay scales. Not surprisingly, women were outraged and started standing up for themselves. They said, "Look! We're not second-class citizens. We want to be treated as equals. Just give us a chance to prove we're as good as any man."

(How ironic! As I've said, historically men have feared women. Men have long been afraid the opposite sex was not only equal but actually superior. In fact, man's effort to keep a woman in her place was rooted in this fear.)

But there's a kicker in this story. Women claimed males and females were equal at work. Equality meant sameness. Sameness implied no differences. Sameness was important because male and female differences at work had become synonymous with stronger and weaker, smarter and dumber, better and worse, richer and poorer, top and bottom. To eliminate this master/slave thinking, women began saying there was no difference between the sexes. "We're equal and alike" was a crucial first step toward equal promotions and paychecks at work.

This was also true at home. Wives wanted to be treated with respect by their husbands. They were not slaves. Male and female differences again raised the specter of better and worse, dominant and submissive. So to right the domestic wrongs women again cried: "We are no different. We're equal and alike."

I think it is one thing not to accept inequality on an economic level at work. Similarly, it is one thing not to accept inequality on a human scale at home. It goes without saying that in a good relationship there can be no second-class citizens. So the "equal" part is long overdue. It is overdue at work. It is overdue at home in marriages where the wives have been treated as slaves.

But it is another thing to say that "equal" and "alike" are the same thing, and that differences between men and women don't exist in our private lives. To believe that men and women do not think and feel in different ways at home is not only false but it also leads directly to a collision course and a series of power struggles over false issues.

What do I mean?

If a woman truly thinks her husband is like her, she'll never understand him. She'll not understand how he can enjoy a sexual "quickie" in the midst of a cold war at home. She'll not understand her husband's desperate need to tune out at night. She'll not understand his feeling that the most important part of his day—making a living—is over when he hits the front door. She'll not understand why he is so allergic to coming close and being more active in the relationship. She'll continue to take it personally. And so will her husband.

If men and women are supposed to be alike, her husband will never understand, "Why can't a woman be just like me?" He won't understand his wife's need for some measure of closeness at night. He won't understand her need to resolve underlying hostilities and make an emotional connection before making love. Indeed, her emotional outbursts will continue to drive him crazy. (While his logic continues to drive her nuts.) And with a mutual misunderstanding of individual differences, the couple will continue their ongoing collision course day after day. Night after night. Year after year.

The trouble is that such misunderstandings ignore the basic differences between this kind of couple. And, unfortunately, they end up getting the pair into the corner of who's right and who's wrong in the relationship.

Almost every week I see men and women who see their particular problems through individual eyes. Being different, however, each partner wants to focus on who's right and who's wrong in a marriage. After years of collision courses, they want to lay blame, assess guilt and place fault. They end up in my office wanting, not a marriage counselor, but a judge.

This is unfortunate. We have to accept that it is not a question of right and wrong, but rather it is a question of what different approaches best suit a man's and woman's differing needs at night.

The sooner we ask what different approaches best suit men and women, the sooner we will have two individuals working their best and hardest cooperatively within a marriage. The sooner we recognize our differences, the more quickly we can put ourselves into our husband's or wife's position and be more understanding; the sooner we can be more accepting, more tolerant of our partner's different needs; the sooner we can all relax and get a little more sleep.

Those differences are not anyone's fault. We have to get away from fault and no fault, innocence and guilt, right and wrong, good and bad. The question of who's right and who's wrong is based on a false assumption that ignores male-female differences. It is the wrong question and leads to the wrong answers.

So again, it is not a question of how a husband and wife can be *equal and alike*. But rather, it is a problem of how a couple can be *equal and different*.

●

*The chief cause of problems is solutions.*

Eric Sevareid

Before I give a prescription for the malady of passive men and wild women, let me add a word of caution. Beware of expert advice. Maybe I can best illustrate that warning with the following story.

Several years ago there was a television program called *The $64,000 Question*. Each contestant answered questions in a category in which he or she had some particular expertise: art, music, literature, etc. The contestants had two choices if their answers were correct: 1) Take the winnings, or 2) Take a chance and double the bet.

Each week there was a series of plateaus which could run from $4,000 to as much as $32,000. Expert advice entered the scene if the contestant wanted to try for the ultimate $64,000. At that point the contestant was permitted to call in and use a consultant.

The apocryphal story goes that an extremely knowledgeable contestant once chose the subject "Making Love." He successfully answered all the questions

87

through the $32,000 plateau and chose to go for $64,000. Consequently, he looked for an expert. And he found that the world's outstanding authority on lovemaking happened to be a man named Pierre who lived in Paris.

On the night of the $64,000 question, it was the program's format to put both contestant and consultant in an isolation booth. So that particular night found the contestant and the Frenchman, who had been flown in for the contest, standing side by side in a glass-enclosed booth, soundproofed so that no hints could be heard from the audience.

As the show began there was much fanfare. Drums rolled. The audience sat forward on their seats. A sealed envelope was brought to the master of ceremonies. More fanfare while the envelope was finally opened. Then, the master of ceremonies read the question over the microphone connection to the booth.

He said, "For $64,000, your question is in three parts. The question is, If you had to make love to the world's most beautiful woman and you had only three kisses—part one: Where do you put the first kiss?" The contestant thought, "That's easy. I certainly don't need an expert for this one." And he answered immediately, "I'd put the first kiss on her lips."

The announcer checked his answer sheet and said, "That's right! And now—part two: Where do you put the second kiss?" The contestant got a little nervous, but he thought to himself, "I've come this far without any help. I don't think I need an expert for that question." So he answered slowly, "I'd put the second kiss—on the back of her neck."

The master of ceremonies again checked his answer sheet and shouted, "That's right! And now for part three and for $64,000!!! Where do you put the third and last kiss?"

Suddenly the contestant fell apart. He broke out in a cold sweat. At last he knew why a person needs an expert. So he desperately turned to the Frenchman and said, "Pierre, Pierre, help me!"

At which point the Frenchman threw up his hands and cried, "Monsieur, I'm afraid you'll do better to answer this part yourself. For you see, I have already *missed* the answers to the first two questions."

So what's the answer?

Over the past decade we've been sold hundreds of answers to solve our personal problems. New solutions, like products on television, emerge every day. We are constantly bombarded with expert advice. The answer is: communication, consciousness, actualization, body awareness, bioenergetics, meditation, nutrition, fitness, liberation, space, "open" marriage. The list goes on. (There is always a key word and, unfortunately, I've now added "passive" and "wild" to the list.)

In one way, I'm reminded of a similar experience during my days in medical school. As fourth-year students we, too, were always given the answer by experts. Every Monday we'd be exposed for a solid week to a new subspecialty. For five straight days a parade of specialists would provide us with the answers about their particular area of expertise. More key words.

Take, for example, the nose.

From Monday through Friday we'd hear about the anatomy, physiology, biochemistry, pathology, diagnosis and treatment of the nose: forty hours of intensive exposure. More and more about less and less so that by Friday we knew everything about nasal passages. In the process, of course, our view of human life was also somewhat distorted. By Friday at 5 o'clock we tended to see men and women as tiny bodies attached to enormous NOSES!

On subsequent weeks we heard about the ear, tongue, neck, breasts. You can imagine!

With today's emphasis on single answers, I think we tend to view human relationships in a similar perspective. We hear about sex, sex, sex. And suddenly, we think of an ideal couple as two small individuals with a gigantic set of genitals. Midgets with monstrous gonads. Or we are told to communicate: talk, talk, talk. And we see a happily married person as all mouth attached to a tiny head and heart.

With such distortions what happens to that special chemistry between a man and woman? Where is room for that private preserve between a husband and wife? What about dimensions we can never really see or know or put into adequate words? Qualities such as courage and kindness, respect and vulnerability. What about decency and commitment and a sense of humor?

The trouble with key words and single answers is that we often lose sight of just how complex a good relationship is. So again, what's the answer?

I don't think "the" answer exists. Maybe the first answer is not to expect a single, instant solution to solve these complicated, long-standing problems.

For example, I do not think the answer lies in a woman's finding the perfect job (which may be extremely helpful for her) or the man's changing jobs (which may be long overdue for him).

For the woman, I think the answers *begin* with her not seeing herself as unique, the only person in the world married to a passive man. After all, she is not alone. The problem is universal. So one answer is for a wife to relax a little bit and not take her husband's passivity so personally.

It also helps for the woman to try to see things from her husband's point of view and understand his pressures. Putting herself into his shoes, she can better recognize his different needs rather than blurring or denying those differences. She can take some responsibility for resolving the problems at home and not just be angry about them.

Again, a wife's pushing and provoking a man to change 180 degrees certainly won't work. However, it does help when she understands that her husband's inner world is often opposite to her own. And because it is different and her husband can't meet all of her needs, it also helps if she can get some of those needs met elsewhere with other friends and, if she's lucky, with other family members.

For the man, I think the answer *begins* with his putting more energy (more work) into his life at home. After all, his daily job takes energy to be successful. Why should his marriage be any different?

Does it not take work to become a successful lawyer? A good tennis player? An outstanding carpenter or electrician? A gourmet chef? An accomplished musician? Should it take any less work to become an excellent husband?

Therefore, the answer begins with a man's becoming more active in his own home. (Actually 10 percent more activity and effort on the husband's part may seem like 100 percent to everyone else.) So even if it is 10 percent more, it means the man must actively assert himself. He must actively talk at night, actively listen, actively ask for privacy, actively fight through his wife's resistances, actively make love, actively express his feelings—positive or negative—in bed or out of it.

Clearly, the answer lies not in a man's always being docile and submissive; his twisting himself into a pretzel at home; becoming a chameleon; being wishy-washy. Rather, it lies in his always being concerned and occasionally assertive; not in his backing down, but in his standing up for himself and his marriage.

I know that sounds good, but let's face it. The reality is that it's extremely hard for most men to do an excellent job both on a job and in a marriage. And yet, I also think that success at work and at home can be related in a positive way. Success in a person's public life has infinitely greater meaning when it is attached to success in a person's private life.

91

What do I mean?

As I've said, there is a basic need for most men to be a good provider, even a hero. Most men still need to go out and do battle, literally or figuratively, and gain some measure of honor, respect and approval in the world. There's nothing wrong with that quest. Indeed, a successful society depends upon such an expenditure of energy from men and women alike.

But the ultimate prize (be it called a promotion or paycheck or creative effort) can be rather empty after the initial flush of success wears off. After all, the roar of any crowd ends after a game. The applause stops when we leave the stage.

The whole point, it seems to me, of being a hero or heroine, of winning the prize, is to have someone to win for. A loved one with whom to share our success long after the tumult and shouting dies. Someone to offer us lasting applause. That, I think, is what makes the effort worthwhile and complete.

This idea is not a new one. In fact, I recently heard Dr. Wolfgang Lederer, a friend and psychiatrist, give an eloquent talk entitled "Love and Redemption in Myth and Reality." He pointed out that in literature and life there is a repeated theme of man's striving to gain approval or "grace." The hero may, in fact, spend a lifetime seeking some holy grail. However, if a man seeks that approval only for himself, he ends up isolated and alone. In spite of his achievements life remains empty.

Whether it is in literature, myth or modern film, the theme is the same. Achievement alone is not enough. Prizes by themselves are empty. In all cases, it is a woman who must ultimately appear in a man's life. She must appear in order to give his achievements a deeper sense of balance, meaning and completion.

In a good marriage it is the woman too for whom the man is doing battle. She is the person who humanizes his life and makes it worthwhile. She has the capacity to balance his thoughts with feeling, his coldness with warmth, his ambition with compassion.

In addition, the woman must play an active role. For example, in fairy tales the beast cannot turn into a prince without the active aid of a beauty. And let us not forget. Should the would-be hero fail in his quest— to turn from a beast into a prince—he is a doomed man. If he fails to find the grail or solve the riddle or win the battle, his sentence is death.

Frankly, I think his being doomed has figurative as well as literal significance. Put simply, the significance is that a man must develop not only his masculine and assertive side, but he must also find tenderness, warmth, love and feeling to make his life truly meaningful. Otherwise he might as well be dead. Most often, and not only in fairy tales and myths, he must find that love from a woman. It is she who will ultimately redeem him.

There is, however, a second interpretation to the same theme. Does not the hero usually go off on his search only to return to the place from where he started? Could not his return home also be a symbol for himself? Doesn't the ultimate answer also lie within him? Must he not find some measure of love within himself for his life to be complete? With this interpretation, the heroine becomes the external symbol for the internal feelings which have been lost or denied in man.

Personally, for men and women alike, I think our finding love, warmth, and approval—without *and* within—is what truly gives an ultimate meaning to our lives.

Therefore, let us—passive men and wild women— learn to accept all sides of our complex personalities. Let us learn to tolerate our ambivalent feelings. Let us not accept easy answers which speak only to one side of our feelings about dominance and submissiveness, dependence or independence, tenderness or tough-mindedness, being a work person or home person. Seeing ourselves in one dimension may be the easy way, but it imposes severe limitations and makes no sense in human relationships.

So the ultimate answer, I believe, *begins* with our refusing to accept the man as passive and the woman as wild, and in our seeing the problem for what it is. Let us accept and even enjoy our basic differences. Let us learn with and from each other what we may have never learned from our own fathers, mothers, or our society: how to accept our human differences and still be strong individuals, active partners, and involved lovers.

All these generalities are easy to suggest in a book. But they're extremely difficult to put into practice. It's like a journey of a thousand miles. And yet, as it was said over 2,500 years ago, "Even a journey of a thousand miles must begin with a single step."

That first step for many of us is long overdue.

# PART V

## Questions and Answers

This section presents many of the questions asked by audiences to whom I've spoken about passive men and wild women. I hope my answers will provide some new ways of looking at an old problem.

## Therapy

*How can a therapist or counselor help a passive husband and wild wife?*

Let's begin with a man's passivity. The therapist can ask: Is it really an expression of *his* being wild and angry?

*Angry? Don't you think a passive man is just tired?*

Sometimes he's tired. Many times, however, he's furious. And I think that a passive man often expresses his anger and fury—which should come as no surprise—in passive ways.

For example, a passive man is asked by his wife to fix the toilet or call a plumber. He agrees, but resents her asking. So he does nothing. He passively resists his wife's request for days, weeks and even months. You might call it sulking, but the result is passivity.

Another example: A passive man doesn't want to go out with his wife to an evening lecture or special event. But he won't actively say so. Instead, on that particular night, he is an hour late coming home or getting dressed.

Not atypically, a passive man gets mad at his wife and won't speak to her for hours or days. Instead of standing up for himself, he remains silent. Isn't silence really the most angry, hostile and deafening kind of punishment?

*Does the man also show his anger in passive ways in bed?*

Definitely. Not long ago it was the man who asked at night, "Do you feel like it?" And it was his wife who had the headache or was too tired. Now it's quite likely to be the man who claims to be too tired.

*Specifically, how can counseling or therapy be helpful to the passive man?*

I think a therapist can give a man permission to have some privacy and withdraw at home. He can be genuinely sympathetic to the husband's needs and assuage his guilt. Here, I am speaking about a male therapist who, like most men, understands what it's like to make a living, provide for a family, be responsible, battle inflation and still keep afloat at home. He understands that these dual jobs are exhausting and that a man deserves to let down. He can support an average husband's natural inclination to come home and relax.

Later, I believe, such a man must gradually be encouraged to express his frustration and anger and need for privacy, if any or all of these things have been crippling him. He can be helped to say what he thinks and feels, and become more active both in bed and out of it.

*How can a man express his need for privacy without at the same time seeming to retreat into passivity?*

Actively and clearly. For example, if a man comes home and he's just lost a sale (or made one), he doesn't want to be hit at the door with, "The car battery is dead," or "The washing machine's broken." He certainly doesn't want to hear on walking into the house, "Let's talk."

However, rather than eating silently through dinner and sneaking onto the couch, he can actively announce: "It's been a hell of a day. Let's have a drink together, but I don't want to live through the horrors of the day again. And after dinner I want to tune out."

Beyond the realities of children's needs and the evening routine, both husband *and* wife are entitled to be clear about their needs for privacy. Ideally, either partner should be able to say, "If it's O.K., I'm going to: 1) Read the paper, 2) watch TV for an hour, 3) go for a run, 4) hide in my room, 5) take a hot bath, 6) be alone, 7) all of the above."

My point is that it is not a question of *either/or*. *Either* communicating *or* hiding at home. On the contrary. A husband and wife should *both* be able to talk together *and* relax alone.

*What about the therapist as an active model for the man?*

The therapist must be an active model. With a passive man he can't sit back and say nothing. He can't passively reflect for a fifty-minute hour like the cartoon caricature of a psychiatrist saying, "Yes, go on.

Ummmmm. Problems? What do you mean by problems?"

*Can you give an example of an active therapist?*

Several years ago in my office I saw a passive man and his angry wife. She was *so* angry, in fact, that she had been having an affair. And not only had she taken on a lover, but she also had told her husband about the other man in her life.

One night the wife's lover had called while her husband was at home. Inwardly, the husband was furious. Outwardly, he did nothing. He told me that he wanted to "play it cool."

When I asked in that hour how he felt listening to his wife on the phone, the husband described being so enraged he felt like a volcano. He thought his head would blow off. He'd erupt at any moment. I asked why he didn't rip the damn phone off the wall. He shouted, "I felt like it!" At which point his wife burst into tears. "I wish you had ripped it off the wall. At least I'd have known you cared!"

*Did such a man's "playing it cool" reflect his passivity?*

You're darned right it did! In fact, I think our language today reflects a growing passivity throughout our society. Not so long ago at school, if a boy was infatuated with a girl, he was described as being "hot for her." To feel passionate about someone was equated with having "hot pants."

Today, if a boy is interested in a girl, how does he describe himself? He says, "I'm easy." He describes his passion as feeling "mellow" and "laid back" and "cool."

*Do most women want their men to be more passionate?*

Without any question.

*What helps a man understand how his wife feels being home all (or part of) the day with small children?*

I know of one wife who finally went off for a two-week vacation alone after five years of marriage. Her husband stayed home away from his job and did all the household chores. That two weeks certainly changed his point of view! He finally understood the isolation a woman could suffer alone with children all day, as well as her need for both privacy and adult companionship at night.

*You've begun by talking about a male therapist for a passive man and a wild woman. What about a woman therapist?*

I think a female therapist can be extremely helpful in such relationships. In fact, she may be more effective than a man. A woman therapist can support the husband and still provide a nonaggressive model for both partners. She can also empathize better with the wife's rage and frustration. In fact, a female counselor might more easily cut through that external anger and tears and get to the wife's underlying sadness and depression.

*Is depression the factor that brings most wives of passive men to your office?*

For both women and men I think depression is the most frequent ticket of admission into psychotherapy. It is true that a wife's anger may seem to be the factor, but it often masks an underlying depression—it is the tip of that iceberg.

*Can psychotherapy treat the woman's depression?*

Definitely. In women and men it is probably the one condition with which psychological assistance can be most helpful.

*Can counseling help the relationship?*

Yes. *If* both partners are motivated.

*What if only one partner is motivated?*

Then, I believe, meaningful changes in the marriage are usually doomed to failure. Frankly, I have never seen a relationship where *both* partners (at least in some measure) have not helped create the problems. Consequently, both partners are needed to help resolve those same problems.

*Does a good relationship always take so much work?*

If there are any shortcuts I don't know them. And not only does it take work, but work for which we are often ill-prepared. For example, we wouldn't think of letting a doctor operate on us unless he'd worked hard and done a lengthy apprenticeship in surgery. And yet most of us marry and have children with absolutely no training whatsoever in being partners and parents. Where else in life are we so ill-trained and ill-equipped to deal with such serious business?

*How common is the problem of passive men driving women crazy?*

In America I think it's no longer just a common problem. It's an epidemic.

*Do you think America's new emphasis on self-awareness will help solve the problem?*

Yes and no.

On one hand, I think self-awareness has been the new frontier. Instead of exploring outer space we have turned inward and begun exploring inner space. The shift has been, in part, a reaction to our being out-of-touch with our feelings. It has been a reaction to our disastrous private lives in which material rewards did not necessarily bring us lasting personal satisfaction. It has been, in part, a reaction to our rising divorce rate, an attempt to improve interpersonal relations.

On the other hand, the self-awareness movement of the recent past has been called the "Me Decade" and America has been labeled the "Narcissistic Society." The names, I believe, simply reflect that a lot of men and women today are increasingly concerned with self-fulfillment and "doing their own thing." They are concerned with *How to Be Your Own Best Friend, How to Save Your Own Life,* and *Looking Out for No. 1.*

My own feeling is that there are two ways of looking at the current emphasis on "I, I, I, me, me, me, my, my, my."

On the positive side: The individual is stronger from this self-exploration and he or she can bring that strength to a marriage. On the negative side: People who turn their eyeballs inward can also stop seeing the other person. With an emphasis on "self" a person can become overly involved with him- or herself as an individual. As a result, commitment, so necessary to a lasting marriage, is too easily lost in this new era of individualism.

*Aside from commitment, what else is missing in most relationships?*

A sense of humor.

# Dominance and Submissiveness

*Who do you think runs most American families?*

As a bride once told me (as her grandmother had told her): The man is the head of the household and the woman is the neck. But remember, the neck moves the head!

*Do you think the neck has always moved the head?*

Not *always*. But it wasn't for a lack of trying. For example, here's a poem translated from the Chinese. In it, the woman laments:

I would have gone to my lord in his need,
Have galloped there all the way,
But this is a matter concerns the State,
And I, being a woman, must stay.

I watched them leave the palace yard,
In carriage and robe of state.
I would have gone by the hills and the fords;
I know they will come too late.

I may walk in the garden and gather
Lilies of mother-of-pearl.
I had a plan would have saved the State.
—But mine are the thoughts of a girl.

The elder Statesmen sit on the mats,
And wrangle through half the day;

A hundred plans they have drafted and dropped,
And mine was the only way.

"The Age-Old Stupidity of Men-Folk"
Written in 675 B.C.

*Who do you think has more influence in most families today—the mother or father?*

According to a four-year study of 2,044 people in the Los Angeles area, mothers were found to have a *far* greater influence on their children's lives. In fact, the only area where fathers influenced their children more than mothers was religious behavior. (If dad went to church, so did his kids.) But mothers were more influential when it came to their children's ideas about religious belief (or nonbelief), law and order, work ethics, militarism, sexual permissiveness, politics and social change.

I think the study documented what we already know from our own experience. Mothers are the leaders in most families. They have more impact on their children than do fathers.

*But you are saying that men should be more dominant in a marriage. Isn't that correct?*

Today, the word "dominant" is both charged and loaded. So it might help to get away from stereotypes and acknowledge that who dominates in a relationship is constantly changing. Not just among the early, middle and later years of a couple's life, but every day.

*What do you mean?*

Let me give a personal example. In the early years of marriage my wife did not work. Consequently, when I came home at night I was pampered, mothered, nurtured and cared for. When our first child was six months old, however, my wife became seriously ill. She was hospitalized for five weeks, and afterward it took another half-year for her to recover.

During her hospitalization and subsequent convalescence, I had to take over the job as mother. It was a job totally foreign to me and, to be quite honest, I wasn't very good at it. But the words dominant and submissive had nothing to do with our life's reality. Was my mothering of our family a submissive role? Or was I being dominant? Did these labels really matter in our situation?

*You've given an example of a crisis. What about dominance in everyday situations?*

Here's another example to illustrate the same point. A husband and wife both work. They come home exhausted at night. They've had it with people and problems. They've had it up to their eyeballs. They're filled to the saturation point. Both partners need to wring out their inner sponge. They need to talk. But the question is: Who talks and who listens?

If the wife talks about her day for an initial half-hour, does that mean she dominates? Or when she listens is she being submissive? Again, do such labels truly matter or help?

*But some men always seem to need to be dominant in their relationships. Why?*

If the man suffers from chronic low self-confidence and self-esteem he may, as I've said, have a compulsive need to prove himself. This need may emerge as a constant desire to be dominant at work, and not infrequently, it also comes out as a desire to dominate women. In a sense, his dominance is really a defense against his fears of closeness and intimacy.

*Don't you think the man should dominate sexually within a good marriage?*

How boring! Good lovemaking, I think, is unpredictable and depends on the mood of the partners. Doesn't who dominates and who submits change from week to week, night to night, moment to moment? In good sex, as I said, doesn't a wife truly want her husband to be active, passive, aggressive, regressive, strong, sensitive, tender, and when she's ready—let loose, go wild and be a little crazy? And doesn't a man really want the same thing?

*Because of the women's liberation movement and increasing assertiveness, are men less dominant and more passive in bed?*

Recently a syndrome has been described called "the new impotence." It is a man's failure to function as a result of the new assertiveness of women, which is so threatening that these men can't perform in bed. Many therapists report this problem as well as an increase in premature ejaculations among American men.

In my own office I hear stories of many women who initiate sex and find the man can't perform in bed. He can't obtain or maintain an erection. Indeed, the harder the woman pushes, the less potent the man becomes.

However, while such reports may be revealing, we also have to use our common sense. After all, if a couple is having difficulties out of bed, so too they will have difficulties in bed.

In this light, there is just as much reason to blame sexual passivity on a man's problems outside of the bedroom (anger, apathy, alcohol, fatigue, the rat race, inflation, indifference, lack of an identity, low self-confidence) as to ascribe it to a woman's assertiveness in the bedroom.

*Do you think a woman should assert herself in bed?*

Yes, if assertion means expressing her passionate emotions. (Most of the time.) No, if it implies putting excessive pressure on the man to perform.

To draw an analogy: Would it help during sex for a man to pressure a woman into having a climax? Pressure just isn't the right atmosphere for relaxing and achieving climaxes. Not for a woman or a man. One simply can't go around ordering an orgasm or an erection.

*But don't some women want their husbands to dominate them in bed and out of it?*

Of course. On the other hand, sometimes a wife just wants her husband to take on more responsibility around the house. That may look like dominance sometimes, but it's not the same thing.

For example, one wife complained that her husband never took responsibility for family functions on weekends. He would lie around on Sunday mornings and never make plans. The wife said, "I just wish he'd announce 'Let's go on a picnic from twelve to two. Then I want to be alone until dinner time.' Any clear statement and decision would be better than his nondecisions. He always says, 'Oh, I don't know. What do you want to do today?' My husband's passing the buck," she concluded, "drives me crazy."

*But you said the same wife may still resist her husband if he gets stronger, takes responsibility and becomes more dominant?*

Yes, I think the wife will often resist. Although she wants her husband to take charge and be decisive, she will resist giving up the control to which she has grown accustomed. She will undermine his initial efforts. But, in one sense, her reaction is a test. And if a man is to pass that test he must fight through her initial line of defense. He must prove that he is not indifferent and apathetic. He must prove that he is strong enough to fight not only for his values, but for his wife.

# Masculine and Feminine

*You use words like male and female and masculine and feminine. Exactly what do you mean?*

Here I would agree with psychiatrist Carl Jung, who felt men have an *anima* (feminine) side in addition to their masculine traits. And women have an *animus* (masculine) side in addition to their more feminine traits. The feminine side embodies tenderness, sentimentality, love, sensitivity, artistry and receptiveness. The masculine part includes assertiveness, aggressiveness and independence.

Jung believed that early in most marriages a man projected his feminine side onto his wife. And the woman projected her masculine side onto her husband. Jung felt a person's task in life was to withdraw these projections and integrate both masculine and feminine sides into one's own personality.

*Do you think there's a difference between a woman's being assertive and aggressive?*

Absolutely. Webster defines these terms as follows:

*Assertion:* Something asserted; a positive statement.

*Aggression:* An unprovoked attack or invasion.

*But how does a man feel today when his wife begins to develop her assertive and independent side?*

Scared. He may feel as if a loaded gun is being pointed at his head.

To begin with, he tends to view his wife's emerging assertiveness as a double-edged sword. At work, for example, he knows that his wife's independence may offer her new opportunities and tremendous satisfaction, as well as extra income. At home, however, he often sees her independence as a potential threat. After all, didn't she once promise to love, honor and obey him? Modern wedding vows aside, isn't it likely that most men secretly want wives who still adore and admire (and not compete with) them?

*What if the wife changes and becomes more independent, but her husband does not change?*

In most cases, I think the man just becomes more and more passive at home. In extreme cases, however, the man (or woman) eventually leaves.

As I've said, most men marry their wives, at least in part, to fulfill a specific need. The man wants an adoring, nurturing woman not only who will be dependent upon him, but upon whom he can also be dependent in turn.

So what happens? His wife changes and becomes more independent, economically and emotionally. With the result that the man is no longer getting his minimum daily requirement of applause and adoration. Subsequently, the man leaves to find a woman who will offer him those qualities he can't (or won't) develop in himself. He seeks a woman who will love him as he is. He looks for the feminine, accepting, dependent, adoring, nurturing qualities that his wife once offered in their early years of marriage.

*What if this type of husband does change and develop his own nurturing side?*

Then, I think he can become more receptive to his wife's needs. He can give her some support.

Let me give a brief example. I know a woman who

combines both dependent and independent qualities. During the day she works extremely hard as a clinical social worker in a nearby hospital. From nine to six she dispenses kindness and chicken soup to a variety of needy people, both colleagues and clients.

Not surprisingly, part of this woman wanted to come home and be cared for. She wished someone would do for her at night what she did for others all day. That someone, of course, just happened to be her husband.

Her anger at home was, in large part, a reflection of that unfulfilled need. She was frustrated at always giving and seldom getting, at work or in the home. She felt there was absolutely no time she could let down. There was no place where she could relax and not bear responsibility.

In this case, however, the husband has been able to change. He has developed the more nurturing side of himself over the past few years. He has been able to reverse roles at home, at least some of the time, and to give his wife the support and caring she desperately needs.

Today, with less anger between this couple, the wife is once more able to give her husband the adoration and applause he also needs.

*Could you give an example of a man's showing both sides of himself to his children?*

I can give you a negative example. It was a case where the father couldn't show his masculine and feminine sides to his own son.

Several years ago I saw in my office a family with a ten-year-old boy. In our second session the boy asked if his father could spend more time at home. Why? "To play baseball with me," replied the youngster. Anything else? "Yes," said the ten-year-old, "I'd like him to show more of his feelings. I never see my dad cry.

And since sometimes I feel like crying it might help if, just once, I saw my father do it."

The father later told me he thought his son was absolutely correct. However, he was genuinely skeptical about his ability to change. It was too hard. He knew he could play baseball with his son. And, quite possibly, he could also learn to show positive feelings more directly to the family. But this particular man honestly wondered if he could ever learn to show a tender or vulnerable side of himself to anyone.

*What about a father showing both sides to his daughter?*

I think it is equally difficult. For example, I have a good friend who is a father and a widower. His only daughter was eight years old when her mother died from cancer last year. Although he is an active businessman, the father does a heroic job with the familiar routine of a single parent: cooking, cleaning, chauffeuring, disciplining, tutoring, as well as making a living. He is, in fact, excellent in these many roles.

The daughter loves her father very much but she has one complaint. She complains that there is no one with whom she can do "the girlie things." (Those are *her* words.) Hard as the father tries, he just doesn't fill the bill. Right or wrong, he never fully satisfies his daughter's need for a woman with whom to do things like window shopping, playing dress-up, experimenting with makeup, and so on.

As a solution, my friend finally enlisted the help of an aunt who lived nearby and temporarily resolved the problem. She now visits her niece on a regular basis and helps to fill the feminine vacuum.

# Identification and Rebellion

*Let's get back to the family with an absent father and present mother. What happens if a boy remains perhaps too firmly attached to his mother?*

Most typically (although not invariably), he fails to resolve his oedipal conflict.

*Oedipus complex? Isn't that an outdated concept in Freudian psychology?*

You certainly need not believe Freud. You can read Sophocles or Shakespeare, who long predated Freud. Both *Oedipus Rex* and *Hamlet* are excellent examples of oedipal situations' going amuck and leading to problems of tragic proportions.

*Exactly what is the oedipal conflict and how does a boy resolve it?*

A boy initially identifies with his mother. During his early years he is dependent upon her. And he is unconsciously jealous of those (siblings as well as his father) who detract from the full attention she gives him.

With his own growth and development, however, the boy comes to realize that he cannot have his mother's undivided attention. He cannot replace his father. Usually, it is at this point the son begins to identify with his dad. If he can become a man like his father, then he can ultimately find someone *like* his mother.

This identification with the father, I think, is absolutely crucial to a boy's development. At some point he must shift his identification from his mother to the father or a father surrogate.

*How is a boy's identification with his father helpful?*

George Vaillant in *Adaptation to Life* reports on the "Best Outcomes" and "Worst Outcomes" of 268 men in the Harvard classes of 1939 through 1942. These men were among the "healthiest and most promising" in their class. They were subsequently studied and interviewed in great depth over a thirty-five-year period.

One parameter of success and failure pertained to an identification with one's father. The conclusion was: "The Worst Outcomes were less likely to have internalized their fathers as role models and more likely to be dependent upon their mothers' external influence." Or put another way: 60 percent of the Best Outcomes had made a career choice which reflected an identification with their father, whereas this was true of only 27 percent of the Worst Outcomes. Also, *none* of the Best Outcomes were seen as dominated by their mothers in adult life, but this domination by mother was true for 40 percent of the Worst Outcomes.

*What if a boy fails to identify with his father and remains identified with his mother?*

At one level the boy may never completely grow up. He may not reach full maturity. He remains basically attached to his mother and often continues searching for a woman to replace her. In transactional (T.A.) terms he remains a Child and he seeks in a wife a surrogate Parent.

*What else can happen?*

Failing to make a masculine identification, some men remain afraid of their fathers. By extension, they are afraid of authority figures (in general) and the masculine side within themselves (in particular).

Men can deal with these fears in several ways. At one end of the spectrum, they can become withdrawn and extremely passive. At the other end, they can become excessively macho. As I've already said, a man's being self-centered, narcissistic and excessively aggressive is one means of compensating for his underlying insecure masculinity.

At either extreme, however, I think such a man's feelings toward women almost inevitably remain somewhat skittish. And his participation in satisfying heterosexual relationships definitely becomes more difficult.

*What about boys who have fathers but don't want to identify with them?*

After he makes an initial identification with his father, a boy can later rebel against him. He often does this as a part of a normal process in finding his own identity. It happens all the time. But, at least in healthy growth and development, I think male identification precedes rebellion and survives it.

For example, let's take the case of a father who is a fanatic about work. After an initial identification with his dad, the son may be unclear about his own future. And yet, he knows that he *doesn't* want to be a workaholic like his father. He rebels. However, rebellion or not, the son must still proceed to find a positive role for himself.

Or let's take the opposite case of a passive father. I recall a wife who told me her father-in-law was a very passive man. So passive, in fact, that during eight years of marriage her father-in-law didn't speak to her for the first four years. The wife reported that her husband had accepted his father's passivity growing up, but subsequently he resented it, and vowed not to be like him. As an adult, he'd become an active parent and excellent husband precisely because he didn't want to be like his father.

*But let's get to the bottom line. Aren't you making a pitch for men to be more active as husbands and fathers?*

Absolutely. I'm making a pitch for the man's being more active, involved and responsible at home. In one sense, I'd like the father to be more of a leader. But I'm afraid that most men aren't willing to assume that role.

Here I agree with Kurt Vonnegut, Jr., who said: "It's one of the weaknesses of our society that so few people are willing to be father, to be responsible, to be the organizer, to say what's to be done next. Very few people are up to this. So if somebody is willing to take charge, he is very likely to get followers—more than he knows what to do with."

## Fathers and Authority

*Why is it so hard for today's father to be an active authority figure to his children?*

I think there are many reasons. Let's begin with a man's work. It has been shown that a man's increasingly flaccid work life has an effect on his increasingly flaccid home life.

*What do you mean by flaccid work?*

114

The *Manchester Guardian* recently reported on the work of a Dan Miller, Professor of Psychology at Brunel University in England. The work involved a survey of how a man's working life affects his wife, children and general personality. Miller divided English workers into two types: bureaucrats and entrepreneurs.

The bureaucrat does one small job in a big organization. He is controlled by a long chain of authority and remains relatively ignorant of the rest. He is a small cog in a big machine. He may work in a factory or university, government department or advertising agency, law or corporation office. Regardless of the job's name, bureaucratic man's sphere of influence is narrow. His decision making is limited. Work and responsibility are split into the smallest possible units.

## What about entrepreneurs?

These men are a dying breed. They tend to work for themselves and are responsible for a broad range of functions. For example, the man who runs a local bakery or laundromat may be an entrepreneur. He may handle up to forty-five different jobs. To do so effectively, however, his work requires that he show initiative, make decisions and ultimately be responsible for these decisions.

## So how does the work life of male bureaucrats and entrepreneurs affect their home life?

Bureaucrats are uncertain and vacillating as fathers. They are less involved, more remote, and liable to defer to expertise or push responsibility on the wife. They tend to pass the buck—to be flaccid. Children of fathers from this type of work structure tend to be more disturbed.

Most entrepreneurs make better parents. They are far more involved with their children. They are certain and active when it comes to measures for their children's welfare. They exercise more real control.

*How are the children of bureaucrats likely to be disturbed?*

To begin with, there is a similarity between this kind of remote fatherhood and absent fatherhood. The children of bureaucratic fathers tend to be low in self-confidence and self-esteem. They are poor leaders and achievers. They have limited vision, and are not likely to defer immediate rewards for later benefits. And, like their fathers, they have trouble making decisions. Not surprisingly, sons of bureaucratic men are also highly susceptible to group influence.

*How widespread is bureaucratic work?*

I think it's everywhere in most industrialized societies. Social scientists describe bureaucratic fathers on the increase in America as well as Great Britain. In addition, as industry in Europe and Asia has become larger, parent styles in places like Germany and Japan are gradually becoming more passive and uninvolved too.

*Are there other reasons for a father's not being able to be an authority figure at home?*

Yes. I think in order to be a reasonable authority figure a man has to have values. He has to believe in a set of "right" and "wrong" values and want to convey that set of values to his children.

*Are you saying men today have no values?*

I think our values are much less clear today. For example, let me cite another kind of father who emerged in America in the mid-twentieth century. He was (to use David Riesman's term) Other-Directed.

The concept developed from the fact that in the United States during the late 1940s and early 1950s we were witnessing a period of unprecedented change and a breakdown in traditional values. Once-stable sources of strength and stability—family, church, neighborhoods and ethnic subcultures—were all crumbling as outmoded institutions.

With fewer models and less of an inner identity and sense of certainty, men began to look outside themselves for worth and validation. Increasingly, a man's identity depended upon external approval and outside applause. Followed to its logical conclusion, these fathers became what I have called a chameleon. He became a man twisting and turning himself into a pretzel to please people. He has also been called a Marketeer and Organizational Man as well as Other-Directed.

*How does all of this affect a man's being an authority figure at home?*

Seeking outside approval for the Other-Directed man is not only a full-time job, it is also exhausting. Without inner values and a belief in himself, he is forever on-stage with other people. He is always wearing a mask with a fixed smile, playing to an ever-changing audience.

Afraid of rejection by the outer world, such a father also fears being rejected at home. To assert his values (which are already unclear and dependent upon other people) means to risk a loss of approval. So this kind of man often becomes another child at home, rather than a father.

*If a father won't accept his role as leader, what kind of men get the children or young adults to follow them?*

There are certainly plenty of negative examples of destructive leaders throughout history who attract large groups of followers. For example, we need only look at

Hitler's appeal as an uncle, rather than father figure, to the young men of Germany.

Today, unfortunately, we are again seeing large groups of young people attracted to charlatans in the absence of their own strong fathers. For example, a whole series of religious cults—from the Hare Krishna to Moonies to the Peoples Temple—has developed under questionable but charismatic leadership.

*But haven't people always looked for strong father figures?*

Absolutely. It's very reassuring to have a strong father figure, especially during times of crisis. History is filled with numerous examples of dynamic and positive leaders who emerged at crucial periods. During our Revolution and Civil War, for example, it was Washington and Lincoln. During World War II, men like Roosevellt, Churchill and de Gaulle certainly filled that role for most of us.

On the other hand, let us not forget that if a child has not had a strong real father, the more desperate is his search for one. And the more likely he is to be converted.

Today, I think we have to ask the question: Why were young people so susceptible to a Timothy Leary in the 1960s? To a Reverend Moon in the 1970s? Or people of all ages to a Reverend Jim Jones as we approach the 1980s? And who will it be in the coming decades if this trend continues?

# Old and New Myths

*What about children today not needing any parent figures? Aren't more and more boys and girls looking inward instead of outward for models?*

On the one hand, of course. In this age of egoism and individualism we are told not only that heroes and heroines are dying. But more immediate to our theme of male-female relationships, we are also told that men do not need women. And women do not need men. Instead, we are told how to be our own best friend. We are told how to look out for Number One. We are instructed on how to satisfy ourselves, literally and figuratively, because we can't depend upon the opposite sex. And if they won't love us, we will learn to love ourselves.

*You've described the old romantic myths of men and women needing each other. Are there new myths to match this era of egoism and individualism?*

Yes, I think there are new myths. It goes something like this: Boy meets girl. Girl meets boy. Both are highly suspicious and even paranoid about the other person. Copulation replaces communication. Sex replaces love. The quest lasts about three milliseconds, maybe three hours, and a kind of mutual masturbation occurs, leaving both people convinced that the old myths are dead. The man believes no woman exists who can give his life meaning. The woman feels no prince will ever come along to discover the princess within

119

her. Both go away from their sexual encounter throbbing and feeling the words from the Rolling Stones' hit song: "I can't get no satisfaction!"

*What would be an example of this new myth in books or films?*

*Last Tango in Paris* is a good example. It romanticizes the ultimate in narcissism. It eloquently shows two people more interested in themselves than in the other person. Both are lonely, isolated and alienated individuals. However, neither wants to make a commitment. No names, no past history, no real feelings are ever exchanged. The only thing that is exchanged are bodily organs and orifices.

Both hero and heroine of *Last Tango in Paris,* after their initial orgy is over, go alone into the sunset. They, too, might have been humming, "I can't get no satisfaction!"

*Do you see any return to the old myths and romantic ideals?*

Definitely. It's hard to deny a theme that is so universal. For instance, in recent films, *Rocky* is the classic example, in a modern setting, of an unloved beast. Rocky makes going fifteen rounds with the heavyweight champion his goal in life. Indeed, he engages the help of an old trainer, a kind of father figure, to help him achieve his prize. But that prize is particularly meaningful because Rocky is going the distance for the love of a woman. (Who, I should add, is something of a frog herself. She even works in a pet store!)

The love story ends with Rocky lasting the fifteen rounds. He gets the crowd's applause (and ours). Yet, it is really the two lovers who provide the ultimate victory. It is not only for himself, but for the love of this woman that the hero has fought. With a battered and bloodied face, Rocky cries out for his girlfriend.

It is her applause that truly matters. She, in turn, runs through the anonymous crowd (and world) with genuine love and admiration for her hero. She proclaims the true greatness of his victory.

*But isn't Rocky an exception? Do you think kids today really buy all that romantic stuff?*

They certainly bought it in the original *Star Wars*. Is *Star Wars* not another modern fairy tale?

The hero, young Luke, is without a father to show him how to be a man. So Alec Guinness in his twilight years must serve as sort of a fairy godfather to the boy. He must teach Luke how to do battle. And if Luke will fight the good fight, Alec Guinness says, "The Force" will be with him.

But who does Luke do battle for? What gives his young life meaning? It is not only to save a galaxy from destruction, but it is also to save that galaxy for the love and life of a princess.

*Do you see any other examples?*

Absolutely. I think that *Superman* is a variation on the same theme. Here, too, a father must teach his son how to use his immense powers for the good of mankind. However, the hero uses those powers not only for man, but for a woman named Lois Lane. Frankly, it's hard to imagine Clark Kent without a Lois Lane in his life. And vice versa!

*Are you saying there's something of Rocky and Luke, Clark and Lois left in all of us?*

I certainly hope so. There had better be. I hope we can get beyond the anger, mistrust and paranoia that currently exist between too many men and women. I hope we can be a little more understanding, accepting, patient and kind toward the people we love.

After all, don't we desperately need each other? Aren't both sexes a little insecure and a bit frightened in today's world? Don't we, men and women alike, need the approval that is so often lacking in our lives? Don't we need all the love and caring, tenderness and kindness that we can get?

*Aren't you being a little corny?*

Corny, perhaps. Romantic, definitely. But passive—never!

# PART VI

---

# Review and Conclusion

•

*We shall not cease from exploration.*
*And at the end of all our exploring*
*Will be to arrive where we started*
*And know the place for the first time. . . .*

T. S. Eliot
"Little Gidding"

The previous discussion about old and new myths has digressed somewhat from my original thesis. Therefore, let us now return to the place where we started.

From the beginning, I have discussed a man who is active, articulate and energetic in his work. But when he returns home at night he becomes inactive, inarticulate and lethargic. He "tunes out," becoming nonconversational, wolfing down his dinner, paying only token attention to his family and then withdrawing to the television set.

Meanwhile his wife, who has been wrapped up in her own problems all day, whether at home or in her career, is looking for "something more" from her husband when he returns in the evening. She wants to talk, to share the experiences of his outside world, to get mental and physical reactions from him. However, she isn't able to spark any of this and, in the face of his retreat, she becomes angry and unhappy.

The easiest conclusion about such people is obvious. Unless the husband and wife put more positive energy into the marriage, they'll get little out of it. No deposit, no return.

And yet does such a conclusion really help us? Is not this similar to one person with a problem saying, "I drink too much," and hearing the response, "Don't drink"? Or someone's saying, "I'm twenty-five pounds overweight," and being told, "So eat less"?

The answer may be correct but, as we all know, the advice doesn't work. It simply doesn't get to the underlying reason why a person has a drinking or eating problem. In one sense, it misses the mark.

The situation is analogous to a runner with pain in his or her leg due to an undiagnosed fracture. Many people can come up with quick solutions: new shoes, arch supports, leg exercises, heat, cortisone, yoga, run more, run less. But nothing helps.

Why? Because to solve an underlying problem, *someone must come along and define the problem correctly*. Someone must say to the runner in pain, "Look, your leg is broken!" When the basic problem is correctly identified, the solutions are obvious and treatment is clear. So too with relationships.

Take the husband who comes home exhausted and regularly reads the evening paper during the dinner hour. There is a plethora of popular advice for his wife. She's told to (1) wear a sexy negligee to the dinner table, (2) ask her husband so many questions that he's too busy answering them to read his paper, (3) burn the newspaper or (4) threaten divorce.

It's true that these solutions may have a kind of rap-on-the-knuckles effect. The wife's action shakes up her husband, and he may not read his newspaper at dinner for at least two or three nights. Then, of course, it's back to business as usual.

In such an example the solutions don't work because the newspaper at the dinner table is not the issue. Like pain, it's only a symptom. Behind the newspaper lies the problem of the husband's privacy at home. Like the runner's broken leg, until the man's need for privacy is accurately defined and alternatives seen, no lasting solution is possible.

Therefore, throughout the book, I've spent a great deal of time defining basic problems which have reached epidemic proportions. If I'm correct in my diagnosis, if I've clearly focused on major sources of marital conflict, then a first step has been taken for anyone who recognizes him- or herself (even in part) as a passive man or unhappy wife.

It is important in defining *your* problems to remember that the key to this (or any) book about relationships is discussing the ideas in it. Few authors, including myself, intend their thoughts to be the final word on a subject. Therefore, use the book's ideas as a springboard to develop your own individual blueprint for change.

Most of those changes will occur in private. However, in focusing on changes in a couple's private world, I do not intend to ignore changes in their public world. Or more specifically, how our society can affect a marriage.

For example, we properly hear about equal pay for equal work but we hear much less about meaningful work. And yet, would not an increase in meaningful jobs also increase both a woman *and* man's sense of self-esteem? In addition to better pay, wouldn't better jobs have a positive effect on a person's sense of self-worth and, therefore, his or her confidence in a relationship?

And what about working wives and husbands who want to spend more time at home with their families?

Where are the economic incentives for doing so? Indeed, how do most couples (with or without children) maintain their standard of living without holding two jobs? With our skyrocketing inflation rate, how does a pair keep their collective noses above water? What are their alternatives in our consumer-oriented society?

The question is, as a nation, are we prepared to reorder our priorities and alternatives? Or are we ready to give up on the traditional family? Are we resigned to serial marriages? Or to no marriages at all? Do we really desire a society in which most people live independent and alone? In short, what do we want and where are we going?

Clearly these are complicated questions and we cannot divorce ourselves from them. We simply cannot ignore the effects of jobs, money, social priorities and public policies on our private lives.

And yet, as one husband said in my office, "My wife and I can't honestly blame our marital problems on the society. Oh, sure, we're all fighting the war for more money and less taxes. But frankly, it's at night, when we either come together or drift apart, that changes do or don't happen in our marriage. So our battles occur in the trenches. Our front lines include things like talking and arguing and making love at night. Those are the nitty gritty issues that are going to make or break us as a couple."

Because I basically agree with this husband's perspective, I'll now shift from a couple's outer to inner world: to a husband and wife's time together in the evening and on weekends. That's where changes do occur in most of our marriages. That's when we need a mixture of chemistry, commitment and good will (most of the time). That's where sacrifices are necessary if we are to achieve some measure of victory in our battle for a more meaningful relationship.

In this spirit I would like to review some earlier

observations and offer a few brief guidelines for the front lines of daily living.

*Define and solve the basic problems with a passive husband.* Sherlock Holmes had a 7 percent solution. I have "the 10 percent solution." As I wrote earlier:

> . . . *ten percent more activity and effort on the husband's part may seem like 100 percent to everyone else. So, even if it is 10 percent more, it means the man must actively assert himself. He must actively talk at night, actively listen, actively ask for privacy, actively fight through his wife's resistances, actively make love, actively express his feelings—positive or negative—in bed or out of it.*

For example, on the matter of privacy, it may take 10 percent more effort for the husband to walk in the front door and say, "Today was absolutely *the worst* day in my life. So DON'T ASK ABOUT IT!"

It takes only 10 percent more time for a husband to help decide with his wife what time they want to have dinner, when to talk, when not to talk, how much television will be watched that evening, who will help with the children's homework and what time they plan to come to bed. Even if these matters are discussed only for a few minutes at night, both husband and wife can then better plan and predict, survive and even enjoy the evening routine.

*Define and solve the basic problems with the wife.* Once a wild wife in marital therapy told me, "My husband suffers from premature emasculations."

Most wives do have the power to undermine their husbands on an intimate level. They have the power power? Does she push and provoke the man to change to support them as well. How does a wife use her 180 degrees? Or does she realize her husband's inner world is often opposite to her own? Does she realize that he can't meet all her needs? If so, can she get some of those needs met from other sources—at work, with friends and with other family members?

*It also helps for the woman to see things from her husband's point of view and understand his pressures. Putting herself in his shoes, she can better recognize his different needs rather than blurring or denying those differences. She can take some responsibility for resolving the problems at home and not just be angry about them.*

She can support her husband in the same ways that she would like him to support her. Webster's defines "support" as follows: "To give approval to; be in favor of; subscribe to; sanction; uphold." As a more specific illustration of indirect support for a man, one divorced wife recently told me that she grew up in a household where her mother always undermined her father. Later, in her own marriage, she found herself doing the same thing to her husband. And for a variety of complicated reasons, the couple eventually separated.

Although she is now divorced and living without a man, the woman admitted that she *still* felt like undermining her husband on occasion in front of her son. At times she wanted to shout at the little boy, "You're just like your father!" But at such times, she vowed to be better in the divorce than she had been in the marriage. So, instead, on these occasions she would run into another room and whisper to the walls, "He's just like his father! He's just like his father!"

*Reverse roles.* I've found that it's extremely helpful for a wife to know how her husband spends his day, and vice versa.

For example, I have seen a wild wife change completely after viewing her lawyer husband during a day in the courtroom. For weeks thereafter she had infinitely more respect for *his* daily pressures.

I have also seen a passive husband take his wife's place for sixteen hours. He began the day by making beds, dealing with the children, fixing breakfast and spending eight hours with his wife at her job as a loan officer in a local bank.

After the bank closed, he then came home, straightened up the house, fixed dinner and handled the kids' complaints. Over the next few months, that day certainly helped the husband better understand how his wife felt when he asked, "How did *your* day go?"

*Actions, not words.* Earlier I mentioned blueprints for change. But it's important to remember that no house gets built by blueprints alone. There comes a time when we must take up hammer and nails. A couple's reversing roles is a good illustration of two people taking an action to change behavior.

It's also important to remember that some of the best actions are the most obvious ones. To use a familiar example, it's estimated by the Nielsen reports that the average American home has the television set on almost seven hours *per day*. Meanwhile, according to one study, an average married couple talks with each other only twenty minutes *per week*.

Therefore, an obvious action would be for a couple to turn off the television set and talk to each other. (By "talking" I mean more than saying, "Pass the ketchup," or asking, "Did you turn off the bathroom light?" I mean two people sharing a wide range of thoughts and feelings, some of which will be mentioned shortly under "house rules.") Even if a couple started talking only fifteen minutes a night, their weekly total might be five times the national average!

The trouble with suggesting such an obvious action is that, once again, it may fail to identify an underlying problem. For instance, when a wife says, "Let's talk," it often scares the daylights out of her husband. It does so because one of her husband's basic problems is that he fears their "talking" will go on endlessly into the night. He does not see a clear start *and* finish to the proposed conversation. Ill-prepared for talking on an intimate level, he feels that he'll get in over his head and drown. Like a poor swimmer who's about to be thrown into deep water, he panics. He can't see the edge of the pool and, without that safety factor, he'd rather not swim at all.

If this analogy hits home, here's a place where the wife can take an action. For example, she might ask, "When can we talk tonight for half an hour?" Then, once a time is set, her keeping to the mutually agreed upon *time limit* is extremely helpful to her husband. It has an edge-of-the-pool effect. Especially for the passive man, it becomes safer to talk. He can relax a bit and feel more in control, knowing that it will not be an "endless" conversation.

*Trial and error.* If you're going to experiment with new behavior in a relationship, there's going to be some trial and error when making changes.

For example, on the subject of talking for a time-limited period at night: I once worked with two social workers who were married to each other. Both were highly verbal people with their clients and colleagues all day, and yet when they came home at night, you could cut the silence between them with a knife.

It took a month of trial and error before this particular husband and wife were once again speaking comfortably with each other on a regular basis.

Another couple spent several months of trial and error just to find twenty minutes alone together on Monday nights. Their eventual compromise was to turn off television during the half time of Monday night

130

football and talk without interruption until the third quarter started.

*House rules.* In addition to the above guidelines, there are also an infinite number of commonsense rules about marriage that most of us hear all the time. However, it's vital to remember that such rules are different for every family. For example, some couples agree at night to "Never go to bed mad." Other couples say on the subject that it's O.K. to be angry, but "Never pick a fight at bedtime." While still others would argue "Never say 'never'!"

The most meaningful guidelines and house rules are the ones which make the most sense to the people living under the same roof. Therefore, I have listed fifty-two subjects which not only provide a basis for discussing house rules. At one topic per week, they also provide a year's worth of subjects for those time-limited discussions at night!

Alcohol
Anger
Boredom
Breasts
Cheating
   (on each other)
Children
Depression
Diets
Entertaining
Exercise
Friends
Frigidity
Gossip
Guilt
Hangovers
How-to books
Impotence

Interests
   (mutual and
   independent)
Jealousy
Jobs
Kinky sex
Kissing
Liberation
Lies
Moderation
Money
Narcissism
Nights out
   (alone)
Oral sex
Orgasm
Pornography
Privacy

| | |
|---|---|
| Quarrels | Values |
| "Quickies" | Work |
| Religion | Weekends |
| Rich people | Xmas |
| Silence | X-rated films |
| Spontaneity | Yelling |
| Telephones | Youth |
| Touching | Zen |
| Ulcers | Zip |
| Underwear | (in the marriage) |
| Vacations | |

*Be specific about lovemaking.* Aside from being specific about making time to talk out of bed, we also need to be specific in bed. After all, sex tends to get boring in any ongoing relationship. One reason for the boredom is that sexual feelings are constantly changing. They change from night to night, week to week, month to month, year to year. What was pleasant last week may be boring this week. What was exciting last month may become rigid and routine this month. So it's critical that we tell our partner in specifics what we'd enjoy during lovemaking.

To draw an analogy with scratching a person's back: We can't do a first-class job of back scratching without giving specific instructions. To really enjoy the experience we must tell the other person: "Right, slightly left, down further, up a little bit, over to your right. That's it. Harder . . . easier . . . there . . . ahh . . . PERFECT!"

So too with lovemaking. And although this is one of the easiest suggestions to make, I know that it's one of the hardest to put into practice. Remember: be specific and expect some trial and error.

*Changes take time.* It's important that we predict there will not be immediate change between most husbands and wives. In fact the higher our hopes—the greater the distance between our expectations and reality—the louder the crash when we must face those realities.

Changes between a man and woman living together day after day are simply not like a TV commercial. We cannot spell "relief" in fifteen seconds or six letters. We cannot take a lotion, potion, oil or pill. We cannot add hot water, stir and get instant change.

Let us not forget that it has taken most men a lifetime to become passive; most women years to become wild. So we should anticipate that it is going to take several months (sometimes years) for each partner to begin changing his or her way of life.

*Ask for help.* If we suspect a broken leg, a doctor can take an X-ray and show us the fracture. To ease our pain, we are given a cast and offered crutches. The assistance is temporary, but it provides crucial support during a painful period. The ultimate goal, of course, is to eventually throw away the crutches and walk alone under our own power.

Although we can't see it on the X-ray, there's nothing wrong with asking for help to get relief from a painful relationship that isn't getting better. I believe the best way to get outside help is to find a reputable therapist. You can ask a close friend (clergyman or family doctor) for names of men and women in your area who have a reputation for doing helpful psychotherapy.

If, for whatever reason, you are unable to get the name of a good therapist, the organizations listed below can be of help.

American Association for Marriage
  and Family Therapy
924 W. Ninth
Upland, CA 91786

American Psychiatric Association
1700 18th St. N.W.
Washington, DC 20009

American Psychological Association
1200 17th St. N.W.
Washington, DC 20036

National Association of Social Workers
1425 H. St. N.W. (#600)
Washington, DC 20005

To return once more to the place where we started and with the above principles in mind: there's simply no shortcut. The man must be more active at home if his wife is to be less depressed. She, in turn, must begin to relax. She must not only put herself into her husband's shoes, but she must also occasionally walk in them. She must better understand the differences between herself and the man she loves and not continually expect so much of him.

As one popular woman writer put it in a recent lecture: "We keep asking our husband if he loves us. He says, 'Yes.' But will you love me tomorrow? 'Yes.' What about next week? 'Yes.' Can I have it in writing? 'Yes, yes!' . . . Can I get it notarized?"

Small wonder that men withdraw.

This is not to say that marriage, active or passive, is for everyone. Clearly it is not. Nor am I saying that divorce is not a meaningful alternative for men and women trapped in a miserable relationship. It is. After all, what could be worse than living for a lifetime in the same house with a husband or wife to whom you haven't spoken honestly in years? What is the last resort for a person who is desperate to change while his or her partner refuses to budge? Professionally and personally, I hear about such marriages all the time.

I also hear many people say that marriage, good or bad, is an outmoded institution. Love is dying and romance is dead. It's the individual who's important. Today we no longer need families or mutual dependence on our fellow human beings. As the twentieth century ends we are not bound by traditional relationships; men and women are now free to stand on their own two feet, independent and alone.

This is one view of life today, but it is only a partial view. Unfortunately, it is the half-empty rather than half-full view of love and marriage, families and friendships.

I also hear that marriage and families have changed enormously over the past several decades. Of course it's true. And they've changed for good reason. The family is no longer needed as an economic unit to farm land and ensure survival. Machines can now work equally well for both sexes. Industrialization has revolutionized our way of life. Traditional institutions no longer provide a stable support system for many of us. We are in a period of transition. Furthermore, our transitional times are complicated by our inflation rate, divorce rate, high standard of living, working wives, television, drugs, consumerism, contraception and our changing expectations about marriage itself.

The inevitable conclusion is that most of us *are* in a state of confusion. Our past is gone and the future is unclear. Constant change raises our anxieties. And as husbands and wives, we often take those anxieties out on each other.

My own feeling is that the current problems between the sexes will not only continue but worsen, unless we interrupt the pattern of passive men and wild women. Why? Because active husbands are already a rare and endangered species. Unhappy wives, much to their husbands' displeasure as well as their own, are on the rise. The result cannot help but have a profound effect on our children.

Indeed, are we not already raising a generation of increasingly passive boys? Will they not create the same problems for the next generation of girls? Whom will passive boys and active girls marry? What is their future as partners and parents? Or is preserving the relationship between strong husbands and satisfied wives worth the effort? Is a meaningful marriage really worth the energy it takes?

To answer that question and as a final conclusion, I'd briefly like to mention another group of patients whom I've also seen in my office over the past few years This group, too, shared a common denominator. However, their common bond was not a marital problem but a health problem. These men and women, who were in their late twenties to their late sixties, had spent several weeks in a hospital bed because of a sudden accident or severe illness.

During their crisis and recovery, these individuals were not confused about what was important in their lives. They were not unclear about men and women and relationships. On the contrary, having faced their own private moment of truth, they had reduced what was crucial in life to a simple sentence. It had nothing to do with power or prestige, money or material possessions. It had to do with restoring their health and revitalizing their most intimate relationships. They wanted to get out of the hospital, recover from the accident or illness and spend as much time as possible with close friends and immediate family. Life was reduced to those few special people whom they loved and who loved them.

Need we wait for a life-threatening event to make such a basic discovery?

Consequently, my answer about love and marriage and families is unequivocal. You're darned right it's worth the effort. The sum of two people in love is infinitely greater than their individual parts. When it works, love combined with marriage can be a cornerstone, a centering experience in our lives. An intimate relationship allows us, however briefly, to see life as it can be lived and to make some kind of sense out of the world.

Therefore, let us—passive men and wild women—learn to accept all sides of our complex personalities. Let us learn to tolerate our ambivalent feelings. Let us not accept easy answers which speak only to one side of our feelings about dominance and submissiveness, dependence or independence, tenderness or tough-mindedness, being a work person or home person. Seeing ourselves in one dimension may be the easy way, but it imposes severe limitations and makes no sense in human relationships.

So the ultimate answer, I believe, begins with our refusing to accept the man as passive and the woman as wild, and in our seeing the problem for what it is. Let us accept and even enjoy our basic differences. Let us learn with and from each other what we may have never learned from our own fathers, mothers, or our society: how to accept our human differences and still be strong individuals, active partners, and involved lovers.

All these generalities are easy to suggest in a book. But they're extremely difficult to put into practice. It's like a journey of a thousand miles. And yet, as it was said over 2,500 years ago, "Even a journey of a thousand miles must begin with a single step."

That first step for many of us is long overdue.

# Notes

## Part I: The Problem

Statistics confirm the picture of a family's spending more time watching television than talking with each other. According to the Nielsen reports 97 percent of all households in the U.S. own at least one television set. In addition, daily TV usage in the average home is currently 6 hours and 19 minutes *per day. Nielsen Television, 1977.* pp. 4, 7.

It is further estimated that by the time a child has reached 18 he or she will have spent 25,000 hours in front of the television set. That is more time than the boy or girl will have spent in school (or in any other activity, except sleeping). By contrast, one study showed that an average American family talks with each other 20 minutes *per week*. Another study showed the interaction between a father and his infant child is limited to 38 seconds a day. See Uri Bronfenbrenner, "The Disturbing Changes in the American Family," *Search,* Fall 1976. p. 7.

Alan Jay Lerner, "A Hymn to Him," *My Fair Lady* (New York: Coward-McCann, 1956).

Joseph Heller, *Something Happened* (New York: Knopf, 1974) p. 99.

For numerous examples of how to communicate about such problems as privacy, support, anger, lovemaking, values and sexual roles, see Pierre Mornell, M.D., *The Lovebook* (New York: Harper & Row, 1974).

Boris Pasternak, *Doctor Zhivago* (New York: Pantheon, 1958).

David Gutmann, Ph.D., "Individual Adaptation in the Middle Years," *Journal of Geriatric Psychiatry,* Vol. IX, Nov. 1, 1976.

For the most comprehensive work on the subject, see Wolfgang Lederer, M.D., *The Fear of Women* (New York: Grune and Stratton, 1968).

The references to practices in Greece throughout the book are taken primarily from Philip Slater, *The Glory of Hera: Greek Mythology and the Greek Family* (Boston: Beacon Press, 1971) pp. 3-74.

Robert Stollar, M.D., discusses the issue of machines and male strength in his excellent *Sex and Gender: On the Development of Masculinity and Femininity* (New York: Aronson, 1968).

*Statistical Abstract of the United States* (Washington, D.C.: U.S. Department of Commerce, 1977). *The Statistical History of the United States* (New York: Basic Books, 1976) p. 457.

Uri Bronfenbrenner, *op. cit.,* p. 5.

Ann Landers delivered her keynote address to the American Association of Marriage and Family Counselors in San Francisco, October 8, 1977.

Bruno Bettelheim, "How to Raise Mentally Healthy Children," a lecture at the College of Marin, Kentfield, California, May 4, 1977.

Probably more than any other character in modern fiction, Joseph Heller's Bob Slocum in *Something Happened* best demonstrates the inner world of today's passive man. Heller, *op. cit.*, pp. 19, 67.

Kurt Vonnegut, Jr., makes a similar observation in *Wampeters, Foma and Granfalloons* (New York: Dell, 1976) p. 218.

"Expatriate Rejects Autumn in New York" by Anatole Broyard, New York *Times,* October 20, 1977, pp. C1, C5.

## Part II: More About Men

D. H. Lawrence, *Sons and Lovers* (New York: Modern Library, 1962) pp. 62-63.

I am aware that many male readers would say the hypercritical parent, if one existed in the family, was their mother. It was her approval they always sought. She was the person they tried desperately to please.

Jung's 1912 observation on the laziness of American men comes from *C. G. Jung Speaking,* edited by William McGuire and R. F. C. Hall (Princeton: Bollingen Series XCVII, 1978).

Kenneth Keniston, *The Uncommitted: Alienated Youth in American Society* (New York: Harcourt, Brace and World, 1965).

There's another side to the same coin. Mothers who put all of their hopes and expectations into their sons also produce men who are extremely successful, at least in their public life. We need only look at a majority of U.S. Presidents in this current century. However, the contrast between such a man's public and private life is often striking and quite another story.

D. H. Lawrence, *op. cit.*, p. 14.

This famous line of George Santayana is used as the opening quote in William L. Shirer's *Rise and Fall of the Third Reich* (New York: Simon and Schuster, 1960).

*Social Indicators 1976,* U.S. Department of Commerce, Bureau of the Census, U.S. Government Printing Office, Washington, D.C. pp. 54-55.

Eric Berne made this remark in a lecture entitled "Frogs, Princes and Princesses." It was delivered at the Langley-Porter Neuropsychiatric Institute, University of California Medical School, San Francisco, California, in October 1968.

Philip Roth, *Portnoy's Complaint* (New York: Random House, 1969).

*Part III: In Defense of Women*

The exact quote is: "Hate is not the opposite of love; apathy is." Rollo May, *Love and Will* (New York: Norton, 1969) p. 29.

Sheila Ballantyne, *Norma Jean the Termite Queen* (Garden City: Doubleday, 1975) pp. 38-39.

All case illustrations combine qualities of people I've known both in my personal and professional life. No similarity between my examples and any one person is intended.

I am particularly indebted to Dr. Alexandra Botwin for her contribution to the section on "Energy."

Edward Albee, *Who's Afraid of Virginia Woolf?* (New York: Pocket Books, 1963) pp. 156-7.

Statistics on American mobility are from the U.S. Census Bureau and are reprinted annually. These statistics come from *The World Almanac and Book of Facts*.

Dr. Victor Beardsley, a psychologist with American Telephone and Telegraph, generously shared both his ideas and nonconfidential research surveys concerning American habits of telephone usage.

Marabel Morgan, *The Total Woman* (New York: Pocket Books, 1975) pp. 21-143.

Germaine Greer, *The Female Eunuch* (New York: McGraw-Hill, 1971) pp. 313-329.

## Part IV: The Problem Revisited

John M. Brinnin, *The Third Rose: Gertrude Stein and Her World* (Boston: Little, Brown, 1959) p. 403.

Jane Wheelright, a Jungian analyst and friend, made an invaluable contribution to this section. She helped to focus on the problem of "equal and alike" *vs.* "equal and different."

The cultural basis for sexual differences is well established. I think one of the most readable and balanced discussions of cultural influences on male-female roles is an old classic: Margaret Mead's *Sex and Tem-*

*perament in Three Primitive Societies* (New York: William Morrow, 1963).

The biological basis for sexual differences is a more controversial subject. However, for the interested readers there's an excellent review article on biological brain differences between men and women. See Sandra F. Witelson, "Sex Differences in the Neurology of Cognition: Psychological, Social, Educational and Clinical Implications," in *Le Fait Féminin,* edited by E. Sullerot and C. Escoffier (Paris: Fayard, 1977).

Wolfgang Lederer, M.D., "Love and Redemption in Myth and Reality," a lecture given in Marin County, California, December 7, 1978.

## Part V: Questions and Answers

Helen Waddell (translator), *Lyrics from the Chinese* (New York: Henry Holt, 1931).

Alan C. Acock and Vern L. Bengtson, "On the Relative Influence of Mothers and Fathers," a paper presented to the American Sociological Association, New York, August 20, 1976.

Morton Hunt, *Sexual Behavior in the 1970's* (Chicago: Playboy Press, 1974).

George E. Vaillant, *Adaptation to Life* (Boston: Little, Brown, 1977) p. 350.

Kurt Vonnegut, Jr., *op. cit.,* p. 246.

*The Guardian,* September 24, 1976, p. 9.

David Riesman, et al., *The Lonely Crowd* (Yale University Press, 1969).

Erich Fromm, *Escape from Freedom* (New York: Avon, 1971).

William H. Whyte, Jr., *The Organization Man* (New York: Simon and Schuster, 1956).

Erik H. Erikson, *Childhood and Society* (New York: Norton, 1974).

Eric Hoffer, *The True Believer* (New York: Harper & Row, 1951).

## Part VI: Review and Conclusion

T. S. Eliot, "Little Gidding" in *Four Quartets* from *Collected Poems (1909–1962)* (New York: Harcourt Brace Jovanovich, 1943).

Nancy Friday was the writer who made this observation in a lecture at the College of Marin on November 8, 1978.

# Bibliography

Albee, Edward. *Who's Afraid of Virginia Woolf?* New York: Pocket Books, 1963.

Ballantyne, Sheila. *Norma Jean the Termite Queen.* Garden City: Doubleday, 1975.

Bartlett, John. *Familiar Quotations (14th Edition).* Boston: Little, Brown, 1968.

Brenner, John M. *The Third Rose: Gertrude Stein and Her World.* Boston: Little, Brown, 1959.

Bronfenbrenner, Uri. "The Disturbing Changes in the American Family," *Search,* Fall 1976.

Broyard, Anatole. "Expatriate Rejects Autumn in New York," New York *Times,* October 20, 1977.

Eliot, T. S. *Collected Poems, 1909-1962.* New York: Harcourt Brace Jovanovich, 1943.

Erikson, Erik H. *Childhood and Society.* New York: Norton, 1974.

Forster, E. M. *Two Cheers for Democracy.* New York: Harcourt Brace Jovanovich, 1962.

Freud, Sigmund. *Collected Works.* New York: Basic Books, 1959.

Fromm, Erich. *Escape from Freedom.* New York: Avon, 1971.

Greer, Germaine. *The Female Eunuch.* New York: McGraw-Hill, 1971.

Gutmann, David. "Individual Adaptation in the Middle Years," *Journal of Geriatric Psychiatry,* Vol. IX, November 1, 1976.

Heller, Joseph. *Something Happened*. New York: Knopf, 1974.

Hoffer, Eric. *The True Believer*. New York: Harper & Row, 1951.

Hunt, Morton. *Sexual Behavior in the 1970's*. Chicago: Playboy Press, 1974.

Keyes, Ralph. *We, the Lonely People*. New York: Harper & Row, 1973.

Lawrence, D. H. *Sons and Lovers*. New York: Modern Library, 1962.

Lederer, Wolfgang. *The Fear of Women*. New York: Grune and Stratton, 1968.

Lerner, Alan J. *My Fair Lady*. New York: Coward McCann, 1956.

May, Rollo. *Love and Will*. New York: Norton, 1969.

McGuire, William, and R. F. C. Hall (eds.) *C. G. Jung Speaking*. Princeton: Bollingen Series XCVII, 1978.

Mead, Margaret. *Sex and Temperament in Three Primitive Societies*. New York: William Morrow and Co., 1963.

Morgan, Marabel. *The Total Woman*. New York: Pocket Books, 1975.

Mornell, Pierre. *The Lovebook: What Works in a Lasting Sexual Relationship*. New York: Harper & Row, 1974.

Pasternak, Boris. *Doctor Zhivago*. New York: Pantheon, 1958.

Riesman, David. *The Lonely Crowd*. New Haven: Yale University, 1950.

Roth, Philip. *Portnoy's Complaint*. New York: Random House, 1969.

Slater, Philip. *The Glory of Hera*. Boston: Beacon Press, 1971.

Stollar, Robert. *Sex and Gender*. New York: Aronson, 1968.

Vaillant, George E. *Adaptation to Life*. Boston: Little, Brown, 1977.

Vonnegut, Kurt, Jr. *Wampeters, Foma and Granfalloons*. New York: Dell, 1976.

Waddell, Helen. *Lyrics from the Chinese*. New York: Henry Holt, 1931.

Witelson, Sandra F. "Sex Differences in the Neurology of Cognition: Psychological, Social, Educational and Clinical Implications," in *Le Fait Féminin*. Paris: Fayard, 1977.